WHAT PEOPLE ARE S.

"Dr. Roger Hall thinks like no one else. The key principles in *DIY Brain* have enabled me to shift my approach to life's challenges and make the most of every opportunity." —Brad Gibson, President, Sound Capital Management LLC

"Roger's ability to take an extremely complex body of work, simplify it while not diluting the message and make it useable for a non-PhD makes *DIY Brain* a top 10 read. If you are interested in changing your industry for the better and being a top performer, this is your book!" —Jason Williford, Master Licensee Culture Index, Entrepreneur, and Professional Speaker, Southlake, Texas

"Who would have thought that a brain book would be a fun and easy read. Roger makes learning interesting, easy to understand and relatable" —Jeff Chilcoat, President of Sterling Sports Management, LLC, Columbus, Ohio

"Anyone who reads *DIY Brain* will have a much clearer idea of how to change their thinking so they can live a much happier life. Roger's ideas and explanations make sense. All you have to do is read this book, follow his instructions, and your life will change for the better. This is a must read." —Kimberley Langen, CEO and Founder, Spirit of Math Schools Inc. (Canada, America, India, Pakistan) and Releasing the Genius Inc.

"A truly great read that is worth every penny and every second. I will be recommending this book to our entire team." —Charlie Kouba, Vice President and Commercial Lending Manager at Bank of Idaho, Boise, Idaho

"In *DIY Brain*, Roger is a witty and worthy guide. Let his practical wisdom change you even if he does have an obvious Slurpee problem!" —Chet Scott, founder, Built to Lead, Columbus, Ohio

"This book is like a checkup for your brain. Roger Hall has a way of making complicated concepts simple and actionable. It's a must read for those who value self-development." —Kristin Tews, co-founder, Noteworthy Media, Chicago, Illinois

"The stories in *DIY Brain* describing the brain and behaviors are both entertaining and memorable. I recommend It wholeheartedly!" —Mike McHargue, President, M5 Partners Principal Consultant, Table Group, and author of *Rookie Mistakes,* Boise, Idaho

"Not only does Dr. Hall effectively utilize the gift of story, but he offers tools for other ideas that include watching movies and listening to favorite songs that allow physical change in the brain neurons. *DIY Brain* is sheer genius and gives exponential value far beyond the investment in cost and time." —Doug Damon, Chairman of the Board, Damon Industries, Reno, Nevada

"This book provides a practical and lighthearted approach to changing behaviors through purposeful mental rehearsal. As an educator, the examples throughout *DIY Brain* helped me to think more deeply about how the principles presented could focus student learning and enhance the students' ability to recognize misinformed assumptions. Enjoyable read!" —Linda C. Martin, Interim Chancellor, The University of Tennessee Southern

"One of Roger's greatest gifts is his ability to tell a humorous, nonthreatening story and hit me right between the eyes. When I have been willing to ponder his insight and do some work, my life changes forever." —Sean Carney, CEO, Specialized Services Group, Inc., Tampa, Florida

"Great book . . . a wonderfully visual guide to bringing change to unhealthy thought processes. Roger's humor and simple relatable examples will stay with me forever." —Bo Carney, General Manager, Specialized Services Group, Inc., Tampa, Florida

"*DIY Brain* challenges the reader to think deeper about the challenges of poor thinking, while offering encouragement along the path to authentic and long-lasting change. Thanks, Roger, for writing a book on a complex topic with chapter titles that drive me to keep turning the page." —Dan Gregory, President, Victory Innovations Co., Hudson, Ohio

"*DIY Brain* is educational and scientific but presented in such a light and understandable way. You are left with an inspiring blueprint for working on yourself to be the person you really want to be." —Dan Stanek, Executive Vice President, WD Partners, Inc., Dublin, Ohio

"Packed with deceptively and astutely combined stories with down-to-earth, unassuming importance and powerful psychological, consequential meaning, *DIY Brain* is designed to change the way you think through stories and humor." —Louis Sportelli, D.C., Practice of Chiropractic, and author, lecturer, and practitioner

"*DIY Brain* is a fun, insightful read that takes advanced, complex theories and makes them easy to understand, apply, and remember. It's sure to be among your favorite go-to books in your personal library." —Jerry Fogle, inventor, philosopher, artist, and poet, Ohio and Florida

"Dr Hall has an amazing talent for communicating complex concepts through stories that are both useful and entertaining. This book is a must read for anyone who has struggled to overcome bad habits or just wants to be a better version of themselves." —Stan Willis, Attorney at Law, Willis, Spangler, Starling in Hilliard, Ohio

"*DIY Brain* is a brilliant work presented in a fun and engaging way. Dr Hall masterfully simplifies an otherwise complex subject, making it so easy to apply." —Brent Oetken, Professional EOS Implementer® at EOS Worldwide, Boise, Idaho

"Some books I read because they're helpful, and some I read because they're enjoyable. This one is both. Dr. Hall has demystified brain science, stress management, and the power of Slurpees—all in one book! *DIY Brain* is the ultimate guide to rewiring your thinking toward success." —Kris Kelso, PCC, author of *Overcoming the Impostor: Silence Your Inner Critic and Lead with Confidence*, Nashville, Tennessee

"Roger's insights allow you to see things you've never noticed before—from the inside out, and outside in. Engaging in the stories and the research will help you truly be a better version of yourself." —Michael Powers, President, Executive and Leadership Team Coach, Upstairs Consulting, Nashville, Tennessee

"Reading *DIY Brain* is an experience that can become a portal to a journey forward to a fuller and more meaningful life." —C. Stephen Byrum, Ph.D., Founding Partner and Chief Content Officer, Judgment Index USA

"*DIY Brain* is amazing. If you want an improved mindset, this book offers practical steps, based in science, to achieving a healthier, happier mind." —Karen Davis, CPA, Green Oak Advisors, Columbus, Ohio

"Roger takes profound psychological concepts and puts them in words anybody can understand. His stories make psychology come alive and make sense in the real world for real people." —Kevin Harris, Herron Classical Schools, Indianapolis, Indiana, and former pastor

"*DIY Brain* is funny, grounded in science, and done in a way that everyone will enjoy and remember. In my work with entrepreneurs and leaders over the last 30 years, I've recommended lots of books. Here's my recommendation: buy this book!" —Dr. Tom Hill, Founder of the Eagle Summits and the Eagle Network

"Success in any field is 80% mindset. You can make your life difficult or smooth by the choices you make in thought, belief, and attitude. Roger Hall presents compelling stories in *DIY Brain* to effortlessly move your life forward." —Patrick Lilly, Founder, REV, licensed associate real estate broker, New York, New York

"Dr. Hall provides actionable insights to improve performance with accessible information and examples. The reader will find his explanation of the complex topics of neuroplasticity and neurogenesis easy to understand and applicable to their daily lives." —Greg Strizek, Ph.D., President, Strategic Analytics, Inc., Falls Church, Virginia

"Once again, Dr. Hall has created a game-changing, mind-altering read. *DIY Brain* takes the complex and makes it simple and practical." —Alvin Brown, author, speaker, and entrepreneur

"In a world filled with so much noise and armchair commentary, Roger provides a relevant, fresh voice. Roger delivers practical and easy to apply guidance in abundance." —Ryan Hartsock, founder of Wild Creative, Cincinnati, Ohio

"Do it yourself does not mean you do it all by yourself. Let Roger Hall and the resources in *DIY Brain* accompany you on a life- and brain-changing journey!" —Mark L. Vincent, Ph.D., EPC, and founder of Design Group International and the Society for Process Consulting, Boise, Idaho

"A must read! Through sharing impactful stories, Roger reinforces the power of storytelling as a leader in creating lasting memories for our team." —Dean Wegner, Founder & CEO, Authentically American, Nashville, Tennessee

DIY BRAIN

The Mindset Makeover Manual for Peak Performance

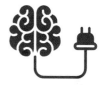

DR. ROGER HALL

DIY Brain
The Mindset Makeover Manual for Peak Performance
Dr. Roger Hall © 2022

Hardcover ISBN: 978-1-61206-260-0
Softcover ISBN: 978-1-61206-261-7
eBook ISBN: 978-1-61206-262-4

Cover Photo Credit: Trish Knapke
Cover Design: Ted Knapke
Interior Photo Credit: Patty Hall

To purchase this book at quantity discounts, contact Aloha Publishing at alohapublishing@gmail.com

Published by

Printed in the United States of America

CONTENTS

Introduction

WHAT YOU'RE
ABOUT TO READ

This book will show you how to mentally connect
things from your everyday environment to
remind yourself to think differently.

Both of my parents grew up on farms. My grandparents were tenant farm-ers. The life was hard, and they were broke much of their early lives. As a result, my parents grew to become relatively practical people. My dad spent his career as a professor of agronomy (the study of soils). As a scien-tist, he had little regard for what I call "hoo-haw." Touchy-feely stuff just didn't fly with my dad. It's kind of ironic that I became a psychologist, a profession with a touchy-feely reputation.

When I was in graduate school, I came home for dinner one time and began telling my dad about what I was learning. Like many graduate stu-dents in the midst of their training, I was enamored with the theory du jour. I can't remember what specific psychological theory we were discuss-ing, but I remember that, about the time we were eating dessert, I made the following statement: "Dad, the trouble with most people is they aren't in touch with their feelings. If people could just get in touch with their emotions and express them, they could solve their problems."

I'm sure he had to work to avoid rolling his eyes when he responded, "Roger, the problem with most people is they are **too much** in touch with their feelings and don't think straight. If they were controlled by their thoughts instead of their emotions, they wouldn't have so many problems."

Perhaps you can imagine what I (the young know-it-all grad student) was thinking. "What does he know about feelings? He's an expert on dirt. I'm the people expert."

The older I get, the smarter my dad gets. He was right. After years of treating people's psychological problems, I have found that out-of-control thinking leads to out-of-control emotions. Errors in thinking really do lead to emotional problems.

This book is about accurate thinking, recognizing erroneous thinking, and the primary importance of accurate thinking in being able to change your life. If your life is controlled by your emotions, then this book can help. You can learn to regain control over your emotions and your life by rewiring your brain and (on a microscopic level) making it grow.

If you have bad habits you'd like to beat, this book will teach you, through mental rehearsal, how to change those habits. If you're the kind of person who has trouble sticking to anything—never fear. This book will show you how to mentally connect things from your everyday environment to remind yourself to think differently. And when you think differently, you change the biology of your brain.

It's not as difficult as you might think. In fact, if you've ever bought a Slurpee, cooked a pot roast, watched an old Western, bought toothpaste, or watched the Super Bowl, then you're well on your way. It's these kinds of regular, everyday experiences that will help you change your thinking, change your brain, and change your life.

Is This Book for You?

There was a book published in the last 20 years that was on the top of all the best-seller lists. For a while, it seemed like you couldn't swing a dead cat without hitting someone who was bragging about reading that book.

Some researchers polled people who claimed to have read the book. Of the 100% of people bragging about reading that book, only 7% actually finished it. If you're expecting this book to be the kind that you brag about reading to your friends, you're going to be disappointed. It ain't that kind of book. (I'd really like you to finish this one.)

This book is written for the regular person who manages a sales team for a window installation company. It is for the owner of a pipeline coupling distribution company. It is for the owner of a set of high-end salons. It is for the hedge fund manager or financial services wholesaler. It is for the homemaker, the entrepreneur, the student, the side-hustle impresario, the business owner, the surgeon, the accountant, and the homeless person (who is right now reading this at the public library).

One of the highest compliments I received about one of my previous books was from a horse trainer. She said she gave it to her truck-driving husband, and he actually read it—and he doesn't read books. If this book is successful, regular people all over the world will be able to change their lives for the better by actually reading it.

(1)

BRAIN 101

By changing our thinking, we can actually change our brains. Start with an understanding of how the **hindbrain**, **midbrain (limbic system)**, and **forebrain** all work together.

Have you ever been unable to shake a bad mood or reacted angrily to a situation even when you didn't want to, as if you simply couldn't help yourself? Emotions can get the best of us—all of us—if we let them.

Right now, you may be thinking, *If I let* them? *I can't control my emotions! They just happen!*

But emotions *don't* just happen. The entire premise of this book is based on that simple fact.

Here is the *SparkNotes* version:

1. Thoughts can control emotions, and you can change your long-term mood.

2. By changing your thoughts, you actually can change your brain chemistry and structure. This makes the changes in your emotions more permanent.

3. Stories are easier to remember than theories or facts. The more you remember and apply the stories, the more your brain can and will change.

4. This little book will help you find reminders for successful thinking in your everyday life—and teach you to connect them to better thinking habits.

In order to make sense of why I am going to tell stories throughout the book, I must first tell you a little about the brain and the cells that make up the brain, which are called **neurons**.

What do you need to know about the brain? Well, it fits snugly in your skull and has the consistency of Jell-O (thus the hard carrying case). It is amazing we know as much as we do about the brain, given that it is so squishy.

What I'm about to describe is a basic model that will make dyed-in-the-wool neuroscientists scream. They'll holler, "It is not that simple! What is he trying to do?" Well, they're right. What I'm about to explain really is overly simplistic. There are lots of other resources available if you want the details (see the bibliography for some of them if you'd like).

The brain has three basic levels. The lowest level is called the **hindbrain**—probably because it is be*hind* the other parts. If you were to put your finger on the spot where your neck reaches your skull, you would be pointing at the hindbrain. It also includes your spinal cord, which goes from the brain to your tailbone. Many bodily functions are controlled by the hindbrain—usually things that you don't have to think about—like breathing, perspiration, body temperature, and balance. Remember when you go to the doctor's office and you get hit in the knee with that little hammer and it makes your leg kick? The doctor is testing for the patellar reflex. The pop from the hammer makes an electrical impulse travel up your leg to about the middle of your spinal cord, and then it zooms back down to your leg and makes you kick. You don't even think about it.

That electrical impulse never even gets to your brain. Your brain is not involved in that response. Fortunately, for most of us, we don't ever have to set a timer on our phones to remind us to breathe. It gets taken care of in the hindbrain—without conscious thought.

The next level is called the **midbrain**. That's probably because it is in the middle. Where is it? If you stick your finger in your mouth and reach way back past the uvula (that hangy thing in the back of your mouth) and up into your sinus cavity, you'd be pointing at about where the midbrain is. You'd also be gagging, but you get the idea. The midbrain contains most of the deep structures of the brain that regulate emotion, and it is also called the **limbic system**. The limbic system has other super important functions as well, but for our purposes, you don't care.

Here is the cool thing. The activities of the hindbrain are re-represented in the midbrain. That means the midbrain can do all the same things the hindbrain can do except in a more complex way, *and* it connects the actions to emotions.

So, let's go back to the leg kick. Let's say a mean dog jumps out from behind a bush, opens his mouth, and lunges at your leg. What do you do? Without thinking about it, you kick at the dog. It's the same action as in the doctor's office; you're still not thinking about it, but it's now governed by fear (a midbrain emotion). The moral of this story? Emotions can limit and control behavior.[1]

And since we are thinking about animals, let's talk about alligators. They are fully functional animals with only a hindbrain and midbrain. They get along quite nicely in life without the next part of the brain I'm going to describe. They find food, reproduce, care for their young (sort of), bask in the sun, and scare golfers in Florida with only the rudiments of a whole human brain. Some people call the first two levels of the brain the "reptilian brain."

The next part of the brain is called the **forebrain**. Why? Maybe because it is be*fore* the rest of the brain. When you look at a picture of a brain, the forebrain is the front of the part you can see. The specific part of the forebrain we want to focus on is called the *prefrontal cortex*. The cortex is

---

1. A word to animal rights activists: I like animals. My household has animals. We treat them well. I do not kick animals. It is only an example. Do not write me angry letters because an imaginary dog gets kicked in this example. I feel better already.

the part of the brain you can see on the whole outer layer. Cortex means "skin" or the part you can see on the outside. Prefrontal means the part at the very front of the brain (right above your eyes). The prefrontal cortex **re-represents** the activities of the hindbrain and the midbrain. In other words, the prefrontal cortex (thoughts) controls and limits the limbic system (emotions) and the hindbrain (reflexes).

Let's return to the leg kick example. Imagine you see an evil person who willfully, maliciously kicks a dog (see disclaimer in the footnote on the previous page). The behavior is controlled at the three different levels of the brain. It's the same behavior as with the hindbrain (spinal cord reflex) and midbrain (emotion), but this time the person consciously thought about it. The forebrain is the part of your brain that controls the thoughts.

Extending the chain of reasoning I described before, the forebrain (thoughts) can control the midbrain (the emotions) and the hindbrain (reflexes).

Let's look at another example: breathing. It is an activity that is controlled by a structure in your hindbrain called the **medulla**. But breathing can be affected by emotion (midbrain/limbic system activities). For example, when you are afraid, you breathe faster. Likewise, the forebrain/cortex can control breathing. I'll show you right now.

Okay, hold your breath.

Done?

See, your thoughts controlled a reflex you don't even think about. You can even hold your breath when you are afraid. Voilà! Your thoughts can modify how your emotional reactions affect your behavior.

This, my friends, is one of my key points.

*By changing the way you think, you can
change the way you feel and act.*

But before you quit reading, there is more stuff ahead that has to do with the basic cells in your brain. You can change them, too!

Neurons 101

The basic building blocks of our brains are nerve cells called **neurons**. These are different from the regular cells you probably studied in biology class in high school. Your regular cells are pretty darn small and look like little ovals. Neurons are also really little, but they are stretched out really long. There is even one in your body that is about three feet long—it goes from the spinal cord to your big toe. The ends of neurons have long "fingers" called dendrites that branch out like, well, branches on a tree.

The cells in our brains communicate through electricity and chemicals—a lot like a wet cell battery. Put some chemicals together in a dish of salt water, and you can get an electrical current. Some basic chemicals (like calcium and potassium) in our wet Jell-O brains interact to create an electrical charge that runs along the length of a neuron. The neurons act a little like wires in your brain, carrying electrical impulses from one spot to another in your brain.

But neurons aren't connected to each other. In fact, they don't touch at all; they are separated by other brain cells (called glial cells) that work like the insulation on wires and by gaps, called **synapses**. These gaps, or synapses, are really, really tiny.

Now look at your arm. Let's say your arm is one neuron and your fingers are the little branches at the end of the neuron. Imagine that your other arm is another neuron, with your fingers being the other little branches. Now, make your fingers interlace together without touching at any point. (Did you drop the book?) This is essentially how your neurons look in your brain (except no fingernails).

Stay with the "arm-as-neuron" picture. Let's say the electricity comes from one shoulder, down your arm, and to your fingertips. Then where does it go? The electrical signal makes your fingers release chemicals into the gap. It would be like little fluid-filled bubbles rising to the surface of your fingers, popping out into the air, and then floating across to the fingers of your other hand. The chemicals, called **neurotransmitters** (because they transmit signals from one neuron to another), attach to the other neuron and stimulate it to pop an electrical signal down its length. Zip! The electrical signal travels up your other arm.

There you have it. That is what happens in your brain every time you have a thought, move a muscle, twitch, blink your eye, feel an emotion, or pretty much anything. It happens quickly and happens jillions of times a day. (Jillion here is used as a technical term.)

You may have heard of neurotransmitters. They have names like norepinephrine, serotonin, dopamine, acetylcholine, GABA (gamma aminobutyric acid), and include hormones, endorphins, enkephalins, and so on. These are the chemicals that pop out into the gap and trigger the electrical impulse in the next cell.

"So what?" you ask. "How does this apply to making me feel better?"

I'm so glad you asked. This all applies because you can change the way your brain is wired. You can change the way these little nerve cells connect and work. That's another one of the big points of this book.

Teaching an Old Dog New Tricks

When you were in your mother's womb, your brain grew at a phenomenal rate, and the general pathways (neural connections) were laid down in the first three months of development. Your brain continued to develop and grow for the next six months, a little slower but still at amazing speed. Then you were born, and your brain continued to grow at astounding rates but a little slower than before. This continued through childhood and into your teen years—the brain continued to grow but at an even slower rate. All the while, your brain has been pruning back neurons that aren't being used, much like a gardener prunes branches that aren't bearing fruit from a fruit tree. The rate of neural growth is much faster than the rate of pruning . . . until you get to be about 25 years old. At this point, the rate of brain development slows down to a crawl and the pruning starts to occur at a faster rate than the growth. For those of you over 25, do not abandon all hope and resign yourself to a life of shuffling around in your bathrobe slurping strained peas through a straw and watching *The Price Is Right*. You have plenty of brain cells to prune—billions, in fact—and trillions of connections between the neurons. Do you feel better now?

The old proverb "You can't teach an old dog new tricks" is not true—you *can* teach an old dog new tricks; it is just harder. Likewise, as you age, it is harder to learn new skills and attitudes because some of the neurons have been pruned. It is not impossible, though.

Why? **Because you are still growing new brain cells and the ones you already have are changing and adapting.** And here is where we have hope (and it's another of the big points of this book). As if you haven't learned enough vocabulary words for the day, here is the last of them: **Neuroplasticity**. What does it mean?

Neuro = *pertaining to nerve cells*
Plasticity = *capability of being molded or shaped*

The concept of neuroplasticity refers to this fact: by thinking the same thought repeatedly, we can change the strength of a neural connection (grow more branches on the neuron).

Okay, I lied. Here is another vocabulary word, but it is like neuroplasticity. It is **neurogenesis.** Neurogenesis means to grow more neurons (on a teeny-weeny, microscopic level, we can change our brain's structure). Our brains are like our muscles—the more we use certain parts of them, the stronger they become. The bottom line is that even though it may become a little more difficult the older we get, we can still learn new tricks. We can change the way we think and thus change the way our brains work.

By repeated rehearsal of thoughts, you can actually change the physiology of your brain. This process goes on throughout your lifetime.

Proof Positive

In a small study in 1996, researcher, psychiatrist, and author Jeffrey Schwartz and some colleagues described an experiment where people with obsessive-compulsive disorder (you know, people who wash their hands 50 times a day and the like) were treated with Prozac (which increases the availability of a certain neurotransmitter) or alternatively, a kind of therapy called cognitive-behavioral therapy (CBT). Essentially, CBT teaches people to think differently.

At the beginning of the study, the people in the study were given a PET (positron-emission tomography) scan. Essentially, a PET scan involves giving the participants a shot of radioactive glucose (ready to sign up yet?). Then they sit under a sensor that looks a lot like an old-fashioned hairdryer that your grandmother sat under in the beauty shop.

Your brain loves glucose and uses it for fuel. The sensor shows where the glucose is being sucked up in your brain—highlighting the parts of the brain that are really active. The computer screen attached to the sensor shows a picture of the brain and the parts that are working hard at sucking up radioactive glucose. Those parts are lit up like a Christmas tree.

In each of the people in the study, one part was lit up because of their obsessions and compulsions (that part is called the **cingulate gyrus**). The cingulate gyrus runs like a little mohawk down the center of your brain.

So, half the group got Prozac and the other half got the CBT, where they were taught to think differently. What do you think happened by the end of 15 weeks? Who got better?

After 15 weeks of treatment, each participant was given another dose of radioactive glucose and placed under the sensor. What did they see? The Prozac people weren't lit up. The activity of the cingulate gyrus in their brains had quieted down. What about the CBT people? The activity in their brains had quieted down, too. The people who had been retrained to think differently had the same changes in their brain's electrical activity as the people treated with Prozac. Their brains were quiet.

When we look at changes that result from CBT, they tend to be a bit more difficult to achieve than the changes induced by Prozac, but the changes in the brain's electrical activity last longer. In some cases, treatment with CBT lasted about seven years before fading. In contrast, the effects of the Prozac tended to wear off once the person stopped taking Prozac.

This early study suggested that by changing the way you think, you can change your brain's electrical activity, chemical activity, and, on a microscopic level, physical makeup. Our big conclusion then is . . . *by changing our thinking, we actually rewire our brains.*

In the last 25 years, since I first began teaching people about neuroplasticity, there has been an explosion of research in the area. Many great books describe with greater technical precision what I've described here. That's not the purpose of this book. If you're interested, I'd encourage you to read them.

The purpose of this book is to help you develop reminders and habits in your everyday life in order to rewire your brain without outside chemicals or brain surgery. You can also rest in the knowledge that your efforts are creating a biological change in your brain that can last!

One way you can make it easier to change a habit is to associate something with the new habit—a mental hook to help you remember your new habit. I call these **Mental Monkeys**, and you'll learn more about them in chapter 3.

Mental Monkey

The next time you go to the doctor for a checkup and you get tapped on the knee, remind yourself that much of the work of your brain is going on outside of your conscious awareness but that with practice, you can control some of it.

Next time you see a bowl of Jell-O (maybe at your next church picnic or family reunion), remember to take care of your brain. It is very squishy and fragile.

The next time you interlace your fingers together, remember that your neurons are like your arms, hands, and fingers.

And the next time you see a tree with a few dead branches, remind yourself that your brain is still growing, even if you've pruned off some dead branches.

Finally, when you hear someone say, "You can't teach an old dog new tricks," remind yourself that it is a lie! It may be difficult, but you can change.

The Magic Act (Write This Down)

What **one** thing did I learn in this chapter that I can start applying now?

_____

_____

_____

_____

_____

_____

What **bad habit** of thinking do I want to change after reading this chapter?

_____

_____

_____

_____

_____

_____

_____

_____

_____

What thing in my life will be my "**Mental Monkey**" (my reminder) that will help me to change my thinking?

_____

_____

_____

_____

_____

_____

_____

References

Amen, D.G. (2009). *Magnificent Mind at Any Age: Natural Ways to Unleash Your Brain's Maximum Potential*. Three Rivers Press.

Amen, D.G. (2015). *Change Your Brain, Change Your Life: The Breakthrough Program for Conquering Anxiety, Depression, Obsessiveness, Lack of Focus, Anger, and Memory Problems*. Harmony, expanded edition.

Begley, S. (2007). *Train Your Mind, Change Your Brain: How a New Science Reveals Our Extraordinary Potential to Transform Ourselves*. Ballantine Books.

Bolte, T.J. (2009). *My Stroke of Insight: A Brain Scientist's Personal Journey*. Penguin Books.

Brizendine, Louann. (2006). *The Female Brain*. Three Rivers Press.

Brizendine, Louann. (2010). *The Male Brain: A Breakthrough Understanding of How Men and Boys Think*. Three Rivers Press.

Davidson, R.J. & Begley, S. (2012). *The Emotional Life of Your Brain: How Its Unique Patterns Affect the Way You Think, Feel, and Live—and How You Can Change Them*. Hudson Street Press.

de Waal, F. (2020). *Mama's Last Hug: Animal Emotions and What They Tell Us About Ourselves*. W. W. Norton & Company.

Doidge, N. (2007). *The Brain That Changes Itself: Stories of Personal Triumph From the Frontiers of Brain Science*. Viking Adult.

Doidge, N. (2015). *The Brain's Way of Healing: Remarkable Discoveries and Recoveries From the Frontiers of Neuroplasticity*. Viking.

Lieberman, M.D. (2014). *Social: Why Our Brains Are Wired to Connect*. Broadway Books.

Schwartz, J.M., Stoessel, P.W., Baxter, L.R., Martin, K.M. & Phelps, M.E. (1996). Systematic changes in cerebral glucose metabolic rate after successful behavior modification treatment of obsessive-compulsive disorder. *Archives of General Psychiatry, 53*(2), 109-113.

Schwartz, J.M. & Beyette, B. (1997). *Brain Lock: Free Yourself from Obsessive-Compulsive Behavior*. Harper Perennial.

Schwartz, J.M. & Begley, S. (2002). *The Mind and the Brain: Neuroplasticity and the Power of Mental Force*. Harper.

Thompson. R.T. (1985). *The Brain: An Introduction to Neuroscience*. W.H. Freeman and Company.

(2)

TARZAN TAKES A HIKE

A story to help you remember how your brain changes when you learn a different habit, plus an introduction to how **novel reminders** and **neuroplasticity** help you form new habits.

If you skipped the last chapter because it looked too much like high school biology and thought you'd rather read about Tarzan, here's the quick summary.

I outlined *neuroplasticity* and *neurogenesis* and how they relate to changing the way you think. To put it simply, if you change the way you think and behave, you can change your own brain chemistry and, on a microscopic level, change the structure of your brain. The purpose of this and subsequent chapters is to give you examples of psychological research that are *easy to remember and apply* so that you can rewire your own brain to improve your thoughts, mood, and life over the long term.

There are several books that address neuroplasticity through engaging in Buddhist meditation, including many coauthored by Sharon Begley. The studies she cites are fascinating and support the power of mental focus on changing the neurochemistry and neurophysiology of the brain. If you're interested in this topic, you would probably find her books quite enjoyable.

In my experience, however, many people aren't prepared to learn to meditate and practice mindfulness in order to discipline their brains. Maybe it's too far out of your comfort zone, too hard to accomplish, or you're spending all your free time watching videos of cats on the internet; we need tools that we can implement quickly and successfully. There are probably other powerful ways to change your brain's physiology. But are you actually going to do those things?

> *Think about it: the absolute best type of*
> *exercise is the one you actually do.*

The same is true for your brain. Mindfulness meditation is wonderful, but millions of people aren't going to do it. So what is left for them? (Abject misery and pain? No!) You're reading this because you want to improve your life.

The purpose of this book is to help the busy businessperson, the hurried homemaker, and the distracted student find ways to change habits of thinking through easy-to-remember stories. Although not mindfulness per se, the techniques I'll share will stay with you. Once you learn them, you can't help but use them.

Changing your brain is like any habit. The more you practice, the easier it is to do. Books like *Talent Is Overrated*, by Geoff Colvin, emphasize *deliberate* practice. Colvin is right. But we pick up all sorts of habits without deliberate practice because our environment cues us to change our behavior.

In psychological terms, **stimulus control** is the process of changing your environment so you can't help but do the right thing. I call it making things "stupid easy."

In addition, there are constant **novel reminders** in our world that prod us toward the best (or worst) habits of thinking.

In this book, I share stories that are easy to remember. When, in the course of your normal life, you stumble on something that reminds you of these stories, they will act as **novel reminders** and without even trying, you'll be training your brain to think differently. By being reminded in the normal course of your day of a better way to think, you'll actually be rewiring your brain.

At this point, you may be wondering what neuroplasticity has to do with Tarzan. Fair enough. Read the story.

Tarzan: 0   Poison Ivy: 1

Suppose you're watching Tarzan out in the jungle. (If you'd like, now's the time you can let out your best Tarzan yodel.) Let's say that the last vine he was swinging on was a poison ivy vine, and now he's itching like crazy. He's miserable and he can't swing for weeks. Now he has to slog through the jungle like the rest of us. Despite this difficulty, let's say I make him go from his palatial tree house to the Crocodile Swamp on foot. How would it go?

Tarzan replies (by the way, it reads better if you use your Tarzan voice): "Ugh. It hard slogging through jungle. There no path. Tarzan get out machete, hack way through. Tarzan cut back small trees, branches, vines to make path. Tarzan dive in big river to get across. Tarzan kill big snake after big fight. On way Tarzan get turned around and get lost. Tarzan slip, fall, and sprain ankle. Tarzan have to cut branches, make splint for ankle, but still have to limp to Crocodile Swamp. Tarzan pretty beat up, cut, bruised, tired. Tarzan no like poison ivy."

The next day, I tell Tarzan to go from his tree house to Crocodile Swamp again. How does the trip go this time?

Tarzan replies: "More easy, but still hard. Tarzan still limp from ankle sprain. Tarzan still itchy. Tarzan still tired from yesterday. Tarzan sore, forgot ibuprofen. Tarzan cut branches and vines and bushes that grew back. Yesterday Tarzan duck under bushes, today Tarzan cut them down. Tarzan still go around big trees, swim through river. Tarzan see big snake but try get away because Tarzan too tired to fight. Tarzan go faster, but it still slow. Tarzan really no like poison ivy."

How about the third day? Sure it is a little better, but it is still tough.

Well, let's say that I am a sadist and I make Tarzan take the trip every day for years.

Tarzan replies: "Tarzan no like poison ivy, but now Tarzan really no like Roger Hall."

In time, he says, "Tarzan get smart, cut down big trees, and make bridge over river. Now no have to fight snakes. Later Tarzan bring gravel, spread it on path so plants no grow back over trail. Tarzan buy shoes. One day, Tarzan rent asphalt-paving equipment and pave the path. Now trip is easy."

Several years later: "Tarzan land big movie contract and buy car. Tarzan widen road. Tarzan now drive from tree house to Crocodile Swamp."

Over the years, because his movie royalties are good (he had a good agent and lawyer, and TBS plays his movies in heavy rotation), the road expands to a four-lane superhighway with exit ramps to the Crocodile Swamp, road signs, and the whole shebang. Now it is easy to get from the tree house to the Crocodile Swamp. It is easy, quick, and takes no thought or effort to make the trip.

Now, because I am really a sadist (and this is all just pretend), I tell Tarzan that instead of going to the Crocodile Swamp, he has to go from the tree house to the Angel Waterfall. It is, after all, a much better destination.

"Tarzan know where Roger Hall live. Tarzan going to get Roger Hall!"

Well, Tarzan has gotten soft over the years and hates to get out of his Lexus with the dbx sound system and the air-conditioned, cool comfort. He's been driving along, Little Richard on satellite radio singing "Tutti Frutti," Jane on his arm and drinking his San Pellegrino without a care, from the tree house to Crocodile Swamp. Now, Tarzan has to go back to hacking his way through the jungle.

"Tarzan no want to do that."

This change is even tougher than cutting the original path because he keeps driving so fast that he doesn't see the place where he needs to stop the car at the head of the trail, until he is already past it. Then he has to hop out, pop the trunk, grab his machete, kiss Jane goodbye (she's no dummy; she's letting Tarzan do the work on his own), and go back to hacking his way through the jungle.

He has to go back to *hard* work. In time, he puts up a flag on the side of the highway and eventually a sign to help him remember where to stop. Then, he cuts a wider path off the four-lane superhighway. Later, he begins to improve this road, and it gets easier to travel down. Then at some point, he stops driving to Crocodile Swamp altogether. He and Jane are winding their way to the waterfall, which is, after all, a better destination.

What happens to the highway to the Crocodile Swamp? *The jungle grows back in.* The weeds begin to grow, and the asphalt breaks up. It becomes harder and harder to go down that path and easier and easier to go down the new path.

Now, how does this apply to you? This is pretty much what happens in your brain when you stop an old habit and replace it with a new one. It doesn't matter if that old habit is cigarette smoking, negative thinking, staying with a loser boyfriend, lying on the couch all day, or brushing your teeth. The process is the same. Once you start a new habit, you are cutting a path in your brain. Each time you engage in the new habit, it is easier and easier to complete the habit. The neurons in your brain are strengthening their connections with each other to make the habit easier to perform. However, when it is time to change to the new habit, it is hard to stop the old habit because you have done it so often. This is true even when the new habit is so much more delightful than the old habit. (The Angel Waterfall is better than Crocodile Swamp.)

Much like Tarzan driving full speed down the paved road when he needs to cut a new path in the jungle, trying to learn a new way is difficult. You often need to be reminded when you are returning to the old habit—similar to Tarzan posting a flag and a sign to remind him of when he needs to get off the highway. It takes real mental hard work to remind yourself to do the new habit. In time, however, the old habit becomes less and less easy to do. In time, you actually have to think hard about doing the old habit—just like the jungle growing in over the old highway. Sure, you could do the old habit, just like you could drive down the overgrown highway, but the road is rougher and harder to take. Instead, with enough practice, you drive down the easier path. The new habit is established. You've cut a new path in your brain. Once you have the new path in your brain (and a better destination), you are less likely to return to your old habit. But beware, the roadbed to the old, bad destination, is still there. You have to keep the road to the better destination clear and maintained so you don't go down the old bad path again.

Your Skull Is a Terrarium

How much is your brain like the jungle? Does it really grow over the old neural pathway of the bad habit? The short answer is yep.

Did you ever hear anyone tell you that you are only using about 10 percent of your brain? Yeah, that is a lie, lie, lie! While your conscious thought uses only a small fraction of your brain's power, your brain is fully and constantly active, doing things you never think about. It's doing things like breathing, balance, and knowing that your arm really is your arm and not someone else's. (Never thought about that, did you?) The other 90 percent of your brain isn't on vacation. It's doing things you never think about.

Even though your brain is fully engaged, it has its limits. (Brain capacity isn't *limitless*, despite the promise of the movie of the same name.) There is a physical limit to what your brain can accomplish—the skull. If you had a bigger skull, you could probably do more than you can today, but the size of your skull is fixed, and your brain is out of room. How, then, do you learn new stuff?

Your brain prunes back the parts that aren't being used and replaces those areas with other neurons that are in charge of other things. Let's look at a really common example. What do Ronnie Milsap, Stevie Wonder, Diane Schuur, Ray Charles, and Jeff Healey all have in common? All are (or were) blind, and all are great musicians. You've probably heard that people born blind seem to have supernatural hearing and sense of touch. (That's the whole premise of the Marvel comic character Daredevil—well, that and a dose of radioactivity.) In Ronnie, Stevie, Diane, Ray, and Jeff, it isn't supernatural. It is just competition between neurons for space inside their skulls.

Think about plants competing for space inside a terrarium. The walls of the terrarium limit how much the plants can grow; therefore, the plants are competing for space in the terrarium. When one plant dies, the remaining ones take over the space in the terrarium. In a similar fashion, your neurons are also competing for the space in your skull.

If you place your hand on the back of your skull, your hand would be over the **occipital lobe**—the part of the brain that is responsible for vision. Your brain has *lots* of space devoted to vision. If, like in our blind musicians, that space wasn't being used for vision, our brains would prune those vision neurons and they would die. That space in your skull wouldn't remain empty; other neurons, like the other plants in the terrarium, would compete for that space.

If you use your hands and trace an arc over each ear, you would be pointing at the **temporal lobes** of your brain. The temporal lobes are the areas of the brain that are responsible for hearing, language acquisition (listening and reading), language production (speaking and writing), and musical ability (pitch recognition and more). In people born blind, we can map their brain activity with a number of different sensing machines. When they are listening, their temporal lobes and parts of their occipital lobe light up. In people who are sighted, only the temporal lobes light up. This shows us that blind people have more brain space devoted to hearing. The hearing neurons have grown in the spots that used to be devoted to seeing neurons. Ronnie, Stevie, Diane, Ray, and Jeff are better at hearing because they have more brain space devoted to processing sound. You and I have musical resolution of about 720 pixels. Ronnie, Stevie, Diane, Ray, and Jeff have musical resolution of 4000 pixels.

Back to You

When you stop a bad habit long enough, your brain starts to use that brain space for other things that it needs. Your good habits are the healthy plants that are taking over the terrarium. Like the jungle, your neurons grow over the four-lane superhighways of bad habits in your head. Like driving over an asphalt road that is broken up by roots, you can go down the path of an old habit. It is rough at first, but you can go back to an old habit quickly because the path has already been cut in your brain. Here is the hopeful part: when enough bad-habit neurons have been replaced with the good-habit neurons in your head, you may find it difficult to return to a previous bad habit.

Changing your brain, your thinking, your emotions, and your behavior is hard work. Sometimes you'll need to post reminders as you're learning a new habit. And not just on the fridge. You'll need to post flags and signs in your mind *and* in your environment that make it easier to do the right thing or think the correct way. If you have a bad habit of behavior or thought, it requires great effort to change.

Mental Monkey

Next time you see a Tarzan movie, remember that with practice, you can cut new pathways in your brain.

The next time you see an overgrown trail or broken up road, recall that once you practice a new habit, your brain will overgrow the old bad-habit paths, making it a little more difficult to travel down them.

The next time you see a Lexus, you can remind yourself how easy it is to maintain a good habit once you cut the path.

Next time you see a terrarium, remember that your good habits are competing for space in your skull. With practice, they will overgrow the space of the bad habits.

The Magic Act (Write This Down)

What **one** thing did I learn in this chapter that I can start applying now?

_____

_____

_____

What habit in my life is a bad destination (like the Crocodile Swamp) that I'd rather not go to but is easy to do so because I have done it so much?

_____

_____

_____

_____

What good place (like the Angel Waterfall) would I like to go to (in behavior or thought) but I haven't yet done the work to get there?

_____

_____

_____

_____

_____

_____

_____

_____

What reminders have I posted lately to remind myself to stay on the correct path?

_____

_____

_____

_____

_____

_____

_____

_____

References

Begley, S. (2007). *Train Your Mind, Change Your Brain: How a New Science Reveals Our Extraordinary Potential to Transform Ourselves.* Ballantine Books.

Burroughs, E.R. (1912/2003). *Tarzan of the Apes.* Aegypan Books.

Colvin, G. (2008). *Talent Is Overrated: What Really Separates World-Class Performers from Everybody Else.* Portfolio Hardcover.

Davidson, R.J. & Begley, S. (2012). *The Emotional Life of Your Brain: How Its Unique Patterns Affect the Way You Think, Feel, and Live—and How You Can Change Them.* Hudson Street Press.

Doidge, N. (2007). *The Brain That Changes Itself: Stories of Personal Triumph from the Frontiers of Brain Science.* Viking Adult.

Doidge, N. (2015). *The Brain's Way of Healing: Remarkable Discoveries and Recoveries from the Frontiers of Neuroplasticity.* Viking.

Ellis, D.B. (1990). *Becoming a Master Student.* College Survival, Inc.

Schwartz, J.M. & Begley, S. (2002). *The Mind and the Brain: Neuroplasticity and the Power of Mental Force.* Harper.

Snel, E. (2013) *Sitting Still Like a Frog: Mindfulness Exercises for Kids.* Shambhala.

3

BARREL OF MONKEYS

To learn new habits you'll need to remember them. How a kid's game can teach us about memory storage and retrieval **because our memories are both fallible and malleable**, with important insights on "repressed" or "forgotten" memories.

Childhood Toys and Memory

When I was a kid, I had favorite toys that I played with all the time—Hot Wheels and G.I. Joes. I could spend hours crashing my Hot Wheels at the bottom of my staircase as they completed the loop-the-loop and flew off into the living room. There was something about crashing tiny cars that appealed to my 10-year-old self. Mind you, it was perfectly acceptable for me to crash my own cars, but it was completely *verboten* for someone else to destroy my toys.

When my parents invited friends with kids over, I introduced toys to these kids in a gradient. Until I could assess the kids' fitness for play, I considered them all to be monsters. I'd start by dragging out a mid-level toy and then sit back and observe. If a careful, respectful play pattern ensued, then it was a Hot Wheels day. If, however, the little ogre broke two levers on Hungry Hungry Hippos and jammed one of the marbles up his nose, I'd bring out the sturdy backup toys. These were toys that I didn't care if they destroyed. It was for such moments that Barrel of Monkeys was made; it's virtually indestructible and only used for play in the direst of circumstances. When the screaming monster child went home with a monkey in his pocket or used the miniature simian to retrieve the marble stuck up his nose, I didn't mind saying, "Uh, you can keep that one. Consider it a gift. Yeah, and the marble, too."

Do you remember playing Barrel of Monkeys? The strategy was only one step short of chess. Take a monkey off the top of the barrel. Use the curved arm to hook another monkey and make a chain as long as possible. Occasionally, if you were really lucky, you'd hit the mother lode and pull up a chain of monkeys that would reach to the bottom of the barrel.

I'm guessing that you probably haven't spent a lot of time thinking about Barrel of Monkeys. But here is why I'm belaboring it: human memory is like that game.

*In some ways, your memory is like
the junk drawer in your kitchen.*

When you remember things, you usually remember things that are easily accessible, like the stuff at the top of the junk drawer. But different from the junk drawer, thoughts are related and hooked together in an associational chain—like a barrel of monkeys. As you hook a memory and pull it out, sometimes it hooks another memory. Every once in a while, it will hook a chain of memories that reaches to the memory that is at the bottom of the barrel. You suddenly remember something that you haven't thought of in years.

Some people call this hooking of memories the *junk box* theory of memory retrieval or an *associational* model of memory. The associational model describes the universal experience of having long-forgotten memories suddenly come to you. They can be as clear as day even though you haven't thought about them in years. Why? Because they were hooked to some other thought or memory in your head.

There is some interesting work and theory about how smells and memory are related. The **olfactory bulb** (the brain structure involved in smelling) is really close to the **hippocampus**, the staging area for memory storage and retrieval. There is some thinking that the stimulation of the olfactory bulb crosses over to the hippocampus and pulls up an associated memory. But let's leave that to another day and another book.

Baby Photos and Dissertations and Quarterbacks

My first real job as a psychologist was at Ball State University in Muncie, Indiana. As I was preparing to leave, they were hiring my replacement. I was brought in to help choose the right person. The person who eventually replaced me was a guy named Joe Abhold. Like most Ph.Ds., he was enamored with his dissertation. Unlike most Ph.Ds., he had reason to be enamored with his dissertation—it was actually interesting.

Here's how Joe got the idea for his dissertation. He was talking to his neighbor (who, as I remember, was putting another piece of tar paper on the roof or side of his house) about his research topic, the distortion of a distant and traumatic memory. Not exactly the over-the-fence type of conversation you'd expect between a Ph.D. candidate and a guy with a piece of tar paper in his hands, but graduate students pretty much lose all sense of social propriety when it comes time to write their dissertations. They are kind of like new parents and pictures of their baby. New parents will grab their phone and show you 100 photos of the same baby lying asleep in the crib while you are supposed to act fascinated and enthralled with the subtly different facial expressions their precious infant makes while slumbering. It is the same deal with graduate students and their dissertations. Fortunately for us, Joe's dissertation is interesting.

Joe was at an impasse. Much of the previous research on memory storage of traumatic events was based on memories that were not exactly traumatic and were actually based on staged events. Joe told his neighbor he needed to find a widely viewed traumatic event that was recorded on video. Tar paper man turned to him and said, "Well, why don't you use the time that boy, the quarterback, keeled over in the championship game and the paramedics had to take him away?"

As it turns out, this exact event had happened five years earlier in the small town where Joe was living, and (fortunately for Joe, but unfortunately for the quarterback) this was one of the most traumatic events that the town had experienced. Everyone in this small town thought their star quarterback was dead in the middle of the football field.

Joe's was one of the first research projects (that I know of) to study a traumatic event that was observed by many people and recorded on video. It was also one of the first to study the perceptions of the people who were actually at the event. Others have done it since with other accidents and other events, but Joe's was unique in a couple of ways.

He was able to show that (1) you can cue the retrieval of forgotten information, but more importantly, (2) **memory is both fallible and malleable**. Joe found a videotape of the event and watched this quarterback collapse dramatically in the middle of the field. Then he found people who had been at the game and asked them a series of questions about their recollection of the event. In the questioning, he was able to insert memories by the way he phrased the questions. For example, "If you had the opportunity, what would you have said to the injured player's father? You could see him, he was standing off to the side, he was wearing a cowboy hat and a *white jacket,* and he was in obvious emotional pain. What would you have said to him?"

(The father was wearing a cowboy hat and a RED jacket, which was a school color.)

And, "Did you think the injured player was going to die during the time when they were *giving him mouth to mouth?*"

(They did not use mouth to mouth at any point. They had used a bag pump resuscitator.)

Later, he asked, "What color jacket was the boy's father wearing?" and "Did the paramedics perform CPR?" Most people "remembered" the white jacket and the mouth to mouth. In reality, and on the videotape, the respondents saw that the father was wearing a red jacket and that the paramedics didn't perform mouth to mouth. Everyone agreed that the boy collapsed, but when it came to the details, those were malleable and fallible.[2]

Dull but Still Forgotten

This brings us to the issue of repressed or forgotten memories. I'm about to share mundane instances of forgotten memories, but by these stories, you will see that it is possible for cues to recall forgotten memories and that memory is both malleable and fallible. The memories don't have to be traumatic either. Run-of-the-mill memories work in many of the same ways.

One morning when I was in college, I awoke from the most vivid dream of fluorescent frogs—the kind you only see in *National Geographic*—teeming over each other in black soil. I didn't think much of it, but it so happened that I was talking to my mom on the phone that morning and mentioned the dream—because it was so cool to have such a vivid, brightly colored dream.

Without missing a beat, my mom said, "Well, you were probably remembering that time in India when we stopped along the road and saw those frogs in the ditch."

"Huh? What are you talking about, Mom?"

When I was 8 and 9 years old, my family lived in India. My mom went on to describe a time when we were on a trip and stopped by the side of the road for a rest under a tree. While we were there, my sister and I discovered a bunch of giant fluorescent green frogs teeming in a dark ditch. For the life of me, I have no recollection of the event. I still don't. However, I have confirmed the story with my dad and sister. Each member of my family cannot believe that I do not remember it.

---

2. In an irony of ironies, when I contacted Dr. Abhold about his research, he had to correct MY memory of his experiment. I wish to thank Dr. Abhold for his gentle and humorous reminder of my humanity and his corrections to this chapter. Thanks, Joe!

You can see that while there is collateral evidence for the event's reality, I had no recollection of it. Somehow, in my dream, the memory got hooked. Conclusion: My memory is fallible. For no good reason, the memory was forgotten.

Let me tell another mundane story. When I was about four years old, I had pneumonia. I was delirious and fell out of bed and cut my chin when I hit the floor. My parents took me to the hospital, and I got about eight stitches in my chin. No big deal, right?

Wrong. Ever since then, my sister and I have been arguing (now more than 50 years of friendly disagreement) about who has the story right. I say I fell out of bed and cut my chin. I also say that for years she believed that I was walking to my parents' room and fell by the bedroom door and cut my chin—and that she only recently changed her story to agree with my version. We currently both agree that I fell out of bed and cut my chin. I was on the bottom bunk, and she was on the top of our bunk bed. We both claim, however, that each has been telling that story wrong for nearly 50 years. We disagree as to who began changing their story. She says that she witnessed me falling out of bed (yeah, right, what was she doing awake in the middle of the night to watch me fall out of bed?) and that it was me who (for years) believed that I was walking to my parents' room, fell, and cut my chin on the floor—and that I only recently changed my story.

Confusing? You bet.

Now look at the collateral data. No one disagreed that I cut my chin. I have the scar. No one disagreed that I fell out of bed and cut my chin. The only thing we disagreed about was who changed the story. One of our memories is fallible (we forget) and malleable (we can change the content of our memories).

To complicate matters even more, my mother (after many years of silence on the matter) swears that I was on my way to go to their room when I cut my chin. Both my sister and I are wrong. You get the picture.

Memory is fallible and malleable. The event occurred, but everyone has a different memory of what happened. With the frogs, I have no memory (and still don't) of seeing fluorescent frogs. Everyone else in my family, however, has a clear memory of the event and each one has a consistent story. With my chin, we all have different recollections of the event, but the unmistakable fact is that I have a scar on my chin.

Why should you care about malleable and fallible memories?

Very often, you will have a disagreement with another person about an event in the past. There has grown a cottage industry of forensic testimony experts in the area of false and repressed memories. Most of us won't have to worry about lawsuits related to childhood trauma, but all of us have had disagreements over how things occurred in the past. In fact, I'll bet most of us want to improve our memories.

When making claims about your memory, it is important that you not accuse another person without collateral data.

Barrel of Monkeys and Memory

Everything I am trying to teach you needs rehearsal. You need mental hooks to associate these concepts with—**Mental Monkeys** to pull the data out of your head. Throughout the book, I will be working to get you to connect a concept with a visual cue, a word cue, or something in your environment. At the end of reading this book, it is possible that all this stuff could be a jumble of ideas in your head. I hope that by associating the easy-to-remember stuff (Barrel of Monkeys) with the harder to remember stuff (the associational model of memory), every time you see a Barrel of Monkeys you will remember, "Oh yeah, I'm supposed to remember about how to pull things from my memory." Because of this (and as you have already seen), we are going to end each chapter with a Mental Monkey—a list of activities or things to look for in your world in order for you to hook the memory and be able to apply it.

Mental Monkey

Every time you see a Barrel of Monkeys game, remember that one memory can pull up other related memories.

Every time you see a quarterback take a couple seconds to get back up after being sacked, remember that your memory of the event is malleable (or can be changed) just by some subtle questions.

Next time you are watching a show about brightly colored frogs, remember that your memory is fallible. You may forget something that is dramatic.

Every time you hear someone talk about a repressed memory, you should remember that you need collateral evidence to support the memory. It could be true, but not enough to convict.

Every time you get into an argument and you are sure that your memory is crystal clear, remember that your memory is malleable and fallible.

Magic Act (Write This Down)

What **one** thing did I learn in this chapter that I can start applying now?

_____

_____

_____

_____

_____

_____

What thing in my life will be my "**Mental Monkey**" (my reminder) that will help me to change my thinking from what I learned in this chapter?

_____

_____

_____

_____

_____

_____

_____

_____

What habit in my life is a bad destination (like the Crocodile Swamp) that I'd rather not go to but is easy to do so because I have done it so much?

_____

_____

_____

_____

_____

_____

_____

What good place (like the Angel Waterfall) would I like to go to (in behavior or thought) but I haven't yet done the work to get there?

_____

_____

_____

_____

_____

_____

_____

What reminders am I going to post to help me remember my new habit?

_____

_____

_____

_____

_____

_____

_____

_____

_____

References

Abhold, J.J. (1993). *The distortion of a distant and traumatic memory: Implications for eyewitness testimony and psychotherapy* (doctoral dissertation, University of Arkansas).

Abhold, J.J. (2022). Personal communication.

If you are interested in Dr. Abhold's research, he can be reached at drjoeabhold@gmail.com

THE PASTOR AND THE $20 BILL

Why stories are far more effective to aid in remembering material than plain prose or results from scientific research. To understand memory, you need to know about the three kinds of memory: **procedural**, **semantic**, and **episodic**. To truly learn something, you must **over-learn** it to improve your performance.

Sunday Morning, 11:25 a.m.

When I was young, I spent a great deal of time at church. Our service started at 11:00 a.m. and went precisely until noon. For those of you who know churches, what I'm about to tell you is completely unbelievable. Hold onto your hats. It was a Baptist church. Yep, it was only an hour, and we never went past noon. I know, right now you're wondering if you've accidentally picked up *Ripley's Believe It or Not*, but it is the truth. For 10 years we had the same pastor. Every Sunday, the highlight of the hour (at least for me) came at precisely 11:25 a.m. After drawing cars on the back of the church bulletin and kicking the back of the pew for 25 minutes (until my dad would look at me sideways), my pastor, Frank Brosend, would call all of the children up to sit next to him while he gave the children's sermon. Usually it would involve a prop or picture or a story. Once he was done, I could leave for children's church and eat cookies. I was big on the cookies. The peanut butter cookies and Rice Krispies squares were the bomb.

Once I got older, I stopped going up with the other littler kids, but 11:25 a.m. was still my favorite part of the service. What I'm about to say next, I want to say very carefully because even though Rev. Brosend has since passed away, he has children and grandchildren. I don't want them to take this the wrong way because he was a good man. In all those years, of the probably 200 or 300 sermons he preached that I heard, I don't remember a single one. I hate to admit it, but I couldn't tell you a single one. But I *do* remember those children's sermons. Many still stick in my mind, but there is one I think of all the time. It is the one about the $20 bill.

The Story

Rev. Brosend told the story of a man who, while walking down the street one day, saw a $20 bill on the ground. He was thrilled to have found the money and resolved to keep looking for similar windfalls of cash. As a result, he'd keep his eyes on the ground, scanning for greenbacks. Over the years, as the man focused his eyes down, his neck and shoulders began to stoop and droop. As he aged, he stopped noticing the birds in the trees, the blue sky, or sunsets. He stopped noticing kids playing in the fields and the kind face of a friend trying to catch his eye. As he looked for more money, he became more isolated. Friends couldn't get his attention, so they gave up trying. He didn't have much to talk about because he never looked around at what was happening in his world. He stopped thinking about the beauty of his world because he never saw it. All he began seeing was crumpled-up candy bar wrappers, black spots that used to be chewing gum, weeds, and cracked concrete. He became bleaker and more pessimistic. In his old age, he became crotchety and grumpy—only seeing the worst in the world—all because one day when he was young he found a $20 bill on the ground.

Now each time I look down and find a penny or a dime, I remember this story. I don't want to become that crotchety old guy, so after I bend down to pick up the penny and straighten up again, I pause and look. I look at the trees and sky and clouds. I look up and notice the beauty around me. I look up and notice the people walking by. And I smile. I don't want to become that man in the story, so each penny on the ground is a reminder to look at the beauty around me and not focus on the grease spots on the concrete. I learned this story, and then I learned a mental habit that occurs as a **novel reminder**. Every time I see a penny on the ground, I remember the story; when I remember the story, I remember the principle.

The basis of rewiring your brain is in remembering stories and linking them to things in your environment (like the penny) to remind you to think differently. As you think differently, your brain rewires.

How is it that I remembered the children's sermons but not the regular sermons? Because the children's sermons were stories. Our brains are wired to remember stories. If we look at how we remember stuff, we can divide the memories into three types. The first is **procedural memory**. This is the memory for how to do things, like tying your shoelaces or riding a bike or brushing your teeth or taking a shower. You don't need to think about it; it just seems to happen.

The second is **semantic memory**, or the recollection of facts such as the capital of France is Paris or the fifth digit of pi is 5 (3.1415926535) or that John Quincy Adams was the sixth president of the United States.

The third is **episodic memory**. This is where there is an event or story that you remember from your real life. Thinking of your first day of school, your brother coming back from the war, or your wedding day are examples of episodic memories. It is easy to forget semantic memories. (Do you remember the U.S. president who preceded Millard Fillmore?) But a story, an episode from your life, well that is tougher to forget. Episodic memory is harder to forget than a semantic memory. Procedural memory is nearly impossible to forget. Just try to forget how to ride a bicycle. It ain't easy.

Here's the problem with lots of personal development books. They teach you lots of ideas and facts, but it is really easy to forget them. Why? Because they rely on semantic memories. You know what I mean: What are the 21 keys to leadership success? What are the five secrets of financial freedom? You can't remember!

Why haven't I forgotten Rev. Brosend's $20 bill story? He turned facts into a **story** and then connected the story to something I experience in real life. He told me (and the other kids) a vivid story that was easy to remember while I was munching on my Rice Krispies treat. And here is the genius: he also connected it to something we all find in real life—money on the ground. It turned from a vivid story to a regularly occurring episode in my life—an episodic memory. Now that I've been rehearsing it for the last 50 years with the behavior of picking up a penny from the street, it is fast approaching a procedural memory.

I realize this isn't exactly rocket science. You can read this book quickly, but if you do, you won't gain the benefit that you could if you read it slowly and reflect on it. I don't just want to sell books (but if you bought this book and are not members of my immediate family, I am grateful); I want to help you make a meaningful change in your life. I want to help you change the way you think, change your brain, and change your life.

This book is filled with stories because you aren't going to remember facts.

Yes, I've provided references to point you to where you can find the facts, but you probably really don't care who did the study and when. All you really care about is the story. It is only by remembering the story that you can change your brain. The next step is to connect the story to something in your real life and rehearse it. Remember the Barrel of Monkeys?

Over-Learning and Piano Recitals

Back in the late 1800s, Hermann Ebbinghaus studied learning. He memorized thousands of nonsense syllables—syllables like "des," "mim," or "vib." (That had to be boring, boring, boring.) Can you imagine what he was like at parties? He determined that he could learn a set of nonsense syllables, but he would forget them right away. In order to remember them

THE PASTOR AND THE $20 BILL

for any length of time, he had to "over-learn" the list. The same is true for all other things we learn. Facts, musical scores, people's names, or the capital of Mississippi. In order to learn a habit, you must **over-learn** it.

If you are or were a soldier, you had to learn how to fieldstrip your weapon. No big deal, right? Once you figured it out, you went on to the next task. Right? No. Your sergeant made you practice it over and over—timed, blindfolded, and while you were hanging upside down from the rafters. Okay, maybe not that last one. The military makes their students (soldiers) practice and practice until habits are **over-learned**.

The military is onto something, just like your piano teacher who didn't accept that you could just get through the piece. She made you practice it over and over until it was practically carved into your brain. You know, she was right. The more you practice a task, the more the practice will actually change your brain. You can't just sit in front of the piano and become a great pianist. A one-time event will not change your brain's physiology; only habits that are over-learned can do that.

There was an interesting study published in 2006 where researchers did brain scans of two groups of people. The first group was made up of experienced piano players. The second group was made up of people who couldn't play piano. While the group members were inside a machine called an fMRI (functional magnetic resonance imaging machine), the researchers said, "Play the piano." However the keyboard was rigged to not make any noise. The experienced piano players knew what they were doing, but the other group just pretended to play.

Both groups showed activity in an area of the brain called the **motor strip**, a vertical strip just in front of your left ear that runs up to the top of your head. This area of your brain regulates voluntary movement. Both groups were moving their hands across the keys. They also showed activity in the **parietal lobe,** the part of your brain that lets you know where the different parts of your body are in space. The parietal lobe is right under the crown of your head.

However, the key difference between members of the two groups appeared in a very different area of the brain. The experienced piano players showed a focused region of activity in the **prefrontal cortex** (right above your eyes). This is the part of the brain that does complex reasoning and problem-solving. It is the abstract thinking part of the brain. The non-piano-playing group showed random activity elsewhere in the brain. You see, while the experienced piano players were focusing their concentration on the piece of music they were playing, the people in the other group were thinking relatively random thoughts like, "I get $5 to pretend to be playing the piano," "This is great," or "This is so stupid," or "I want a cheeseburger."

Here is where it gets interesting. The researchers then told the people in the two groups to sit quietly and listen to music. While the non-musicians were imagining random thoughts like, "Hey, maybe I can use the $5 to buy a cheeseburger," or, "I like this song—I wonder what it is called," the pianists, figuratively sitting on their hands, imagined playing the piano. The motor strip was quiet for the non-musicians but lit up for the experienced piano players while they sat still. In addition, the pianists showed the same concentrated activity in their prefrontal cortex that they had while they were playing the piece without hearing the sound. While they were listening to the music, they were pretending to play it. Their mental rehearsal without action was creating the same brain activity that actual practice had created.

Mental Rehearsal and Olympians

What we are discovering is that mental rehearsal of a behavior or repeated mental rehearsal of a thought habit actually changes your brain's physiology. Sports psychologists have been doing this for years with their athletes. A colleague of mine, Chris Carr, has worked with the U.S. Olympic ski team. He'd have the downhill skiers scout the hill and then mentally rehearse their run. The more they mentally rehearsed the route, the better they did. By mentally rehearsing, they were more likely to succeed when they actually did the run.

Mental rehearsal is not fun. In fact, it can be pretty dull. If you were ever on a basketball team, your coach made you run wind sprints. No one does wind sprints for their own sake. Wind sprints never won a basketball game. Only baskets win basketball games, but the wind sprints in practice lead to endurance. That endurance allows the player to stay in the game and make baskets at the end of the second half when the competition is sucking wind. Practicing mental habits and gaining mental discipline isn't fun, but changing your brain's physiology requires it.

Benefiting from this book will only occur if you practice the mental habits. My goal is to make these mental habits more palatable to perform. I'm trying to make the wind sprints more fun. That is why I, dear reader, am trying to associate these concepts with stories. You'll probably never remember who did which study or many of the details—and frankly I don't care if you do. The stories, like Rev. Brosend's children's sermons, will come to mind more easily. They will be pulled when you associate them with something in your environment, just like I associated picking up a penny with appreciating the beauty around me.

In the Mental Monkey section at the end of each chapter, I encourage you to associate an object or action in your regular environment with the stories you've read (which will, I hope, turn it into episodic memory). That physical reminder in your environment can then remind you to change your thinking, rewire your brain, and change your life. This is "do-it-yourself" brain.

Mental Monkey

 Next time you are in church, listen closely to the children's sermon. In 20 years, the story may be the only thing you remember from the service.

 Next time you see someone practice the piano, remember that by rehearsing and over-learning, you can change your brain's physiology.

 Next time you are running wind sprints and cursing at your coach under your breath—or doing any kind of rigorous, exhausting exercise—remember that your brain needs the same kind of rehearsal to rewire itself.

 When you see a penny on the ground and pick it up, remember to look to the sky and the trees. Remember to enjoy the beauty of the world. Remember each time you pick up a penny that you can discipline your thinking and change your brain.

The Magic Act (Write This Down)

What **one** thing did I learn in this chapter that I can start applying now?

_____

_____

_____

_____

_____

What **bad habit** of thinking do I want to change after reading this chapter?

_____

_____

_____

_____

_____

_____

_____

What thing in my life will be my "**Mental Monkey**" (my reminder) that will help me to change my thinking from what I learned in this chapter?

_____

_____

_____

_____

_____

_____

_____

_____

What good place (like the Angel Waterfall) would I like to go to (in behavior or thought) but I haven't yet done the work to get there?

_____

_____

_____

_____

_____

_____

_____

What reminders am I going to post to help me remember my new habit?

_____

_____

_____

_____

_____

_____

_____

_____

_____

References

https://www.psychologytoday.com/us/basics/memory/types-memory

https://en.wikipedia.org/wiki/Hermann_Ebbinghaus

Bangert, M., Peschel, T., Schlaug, G., Rotte, M., Drescher, D., Hinrichs, H., Heinze, H.J. & Altenmüller, E. (2006). Shared networks for auditory and motor processing in professional pianists: evidence from fMRI conjunction. *Neuroimage*, *30*(3), 917-926.

Carr, C. "Sport Psychology: Psychological Concepts and Interventions," chapter 2, pp. 11-16, within Buschbacher, M.D., R.M., Prahlow, M.D., N.D. & Dave, D.O., S. J. (2008). *Sports Medicine and Rehabilitation: A Sport-specific Approach, Second Edition.* Lippincott Williams & Wilkins.

Carr, C. (1999). Personal communication.

Cron, L. (2012). *Wired for Story: The Writer's Guide to Using Brain Science to Hook Readers from the Very First Sentence.* Ten Speed Press.

Gaser, C. & Schlaug, G. (2003). Brain structures differ between musicians and non-musicians. *Journal of Neuroscience*, *23*(27), 9240-9245.

Haueisen, J. & Knösche, T.R. (2001). Involuntary motor activity in pianists evoked by music perception. *Journal of Cognitive Neuroscience*, *13*(6), 786-792.

Hund-Georgiadis, M. & Von Cramon, D.Y. (1999). Motor-learning-related changes in piano players and non-musicians revealed by functional magnetic resonance signals. *Experimental Brain Research*, *125*(4), 417-425.

Jäncke, L., Shah, N.J. & Peters, M. (2000). Cortical activations in primary and secondary motor areas for complex bimanual movements in professional pianists. *Cognitive Brain Research*, *10*(1-2), 177-183.

Krings, T., Töpper, R., Foltys, H., Erberich, S., Sparing, R., Willmes, K. & Thron, A. (2000). Cortical activation patterns during complex motor tasks in piano players and control subjects. A functional magnetic resonance imaging study. *Neuroscience Letters*, *278*(3), 189-193.

Meister, I.G., Krings, T., Foltys, H., Boroojerdi, B., Müller, M., Töpper, R. & Thron, A. (2004). Playing piano in the mind—an fMRI study on music imagery and performance in pianists. *Cognitive Brain Research*, *19*(3), 219-228.

Münte, T.F., Altenmüller, E. & Jäncke, L. (2002). The musician's brain as a model of neuroplasticity. *Nature Reviews Neuroscience*, *3*(6), 473-478.

Ohnishi, T. (2001). Functional anatomy of musical perception in musicians. *Cerebral Cortex*, *11*(8), 754-760.

Pantev, C., Oostenveld, R., Engelien, A., Ross, B., Roberts, L.E. & Hoke, M. (1998). Increased auditory cortical representation in musicians. *Nature*, *392*(6678), 811-814.

Schlaug, G. (2001). The brain of musicians: A model for functional and structural adaptation. *Annals of the New York Academy of Sciences*, *930*(1), 281-299.

Schlaug, G., Jäncke, L., Huang, Y. & Steinmetz, H. (1995). In vivo evidence of structural brain asymmetry in musicians. *Science*, *267*(5198), 699-701.

(5)

DENTAL HYGIENIST HUMILIATION

How my trip to the dentist will help you understand why it is so difficult to change a habit. To do the hard work of modifying your old habits, you need at least three ways to help you: **novel reminders**, **irritating reminders**, and **stimulus control**.

"Men acquire a particular quality by constantly acting in a particular way."

—Aristotle (384 B.C.–322 B.C.)

"Such as are your habitual thoughts, such also will be the character of your mind; for the soul is dyed by the thoughts."

—Marcus Aurelius Antoninus (A.D. 121– A.D. 180)

A Habit That Might Have Changed World War II

In 1931, two years before Hitler would become Chancellor of Germany, Winston Churchill, a British statesman, was on a speaking tour of the United States. He was crossing the street in New York City. In the U.S., cars drive on the right side of the road. In the U.K., Japan, lots of the rest of Asia, and dozens of former British colonies, they drive on the left-hand side of the road.

If you are in a country that drives on the right side of the road, when you are crossing the street, you look left, right, left. In the U.K., it's right, left, right. When Winston Churchill stepped off that curb in New York City, his lifetime habit of right, left, right, nearly got him killed. He looked both ways in the wrong order, stepped out and was hit by a cab. His deeply ingrained right, left, right looking nearly got him killed. If he had died, I wonder what would have happened in World War II. Our habits can have far-reaching implications.

Churchill's habit was a good one applied in the wrong situation. We all know we have bad habits that we'd like to change. We try and fail and get discouraged. Sometimes professional consultants don't help either.

Lies Consultants Tell

They lie. Consultants tell dramatic lies to make a point. I am a consultant, so I'm not throwing the rest of my class under the bus. I am also guilty of telling vivid stories to drive a point home that may have a dubious connection to reality. Over the last 30 years, I hope I've learned to introduce such a story with the phrase, "This may not be true, but it is such a good story I tell it anyway." Here is one of my favorite consultant lies.

"It only takes 28 days to learn a new habit."

This, my friends, is a lie from the pit of hell. It just ain't true.

Before smartphones, mobile phones had a tiny little screen with physical buttons. In fact, all phones had physical buttons (and a really long time ago they had dials). Except when you were sitting on the school bus drawing pictures in the fog on the windows, you had no previous experience interacting with a piece of glass. And I don't mean licking it. When you got your first smartphone, how long did it take you to interact with that piece of glass?

Most people tell me they figured it out within a couple of days. Most of us learned to thumb type on a piece of glass within a week. What does that tell us? It doesn't take 28 days to learn a new habit. Shoot, you can learn a new habit within 48 hours—EXCEPT that if you are an adult, you aren't learning new habits. You're replacing old, ingrained habits with very similar new habits and this, my friends, takes a LONG time. If you want to unlearn a habit, it's very difficult, very difficult.

Changing old, ingrained habits is exceedingly difficult.

Guilt and Shame 101

Let me give you an example. When I was 33, I went to the dentist to get my teeth cleaned. I've had them cleaned since then, but I tell you about my age at the time for a reason. There I was, sitting in the dental chair, wearing a plastic lavender bib hooked around my neck with a metal cable and two alligator clips. The dental hygienist had her finger hooked in the corner of my mouth and the other hand on her hip.

She tilted her head, looked at me, and said, "You know, I can tell by the way the plaque is built up on your teeth that you're a scrubber."

I looked at her and said "Okay, I'm busted. I'm a scrubber. I admit it and I'm bad about flossing, too."

Then she said, "You know, you need to brush in little circles."

And I said "Okay, I got it. Locked in my mind. I'm good to go. Thanks!"

She removed her finger from the corner of my mouth and held it up, "Wait a second." She turned around and rummaged around in the cupboard and pulled out the giant set of fake teeth and the giant toothbrush—the kind they show the kids when they are in the 3rd grade—and she held it up to me.

With her left arm curled around the giant teeth and her right hand on the giant red toothbrush, she started to demonstrate: "See, you scrub back and forth like this, left right left with the brush. What you want to do is make little circles to get up underneath the gum line and get the plaque out. We don't want you getting gum disease. You don't want to go to the periodontist, do you?"

The blood was beginning to rise into my face. To which I responded, "Yep, I've got it. I'm with you. Got it a hundred percent. Little circles. I'm good, thanks. Nope, I don't want to go to the periodontist. Thanks!"

Then she actually handed me the giant fake teeth and the big toothbrush and said, "You do it for me."

So there I was, 33 years old, sitting in a dentist's chair, wearing a lavender bib and with a set of giant fake teeth and an outsized toothbrush in my hands, making little circles. (I am convinced that in dental hygienist school, they have a class called "Inducing Guilt and Shame 101." I'm sure she got an A and took the advanced class, "Refined Techniques for Inducing Guilt and Shame 201.")[3]

So that night, when I got home, filled with guilt and shame, I brushed my teeth, making little circles. There I was: circle, circle, circle, spit. Circle, circle, circle, spit. Done.

Next morning, I woke up. Circle, circle, circle, spit. I looked at my watch. *Oh crap, I'm late.* Scrub, scrub, scrub, spit, and I'm done.

That night, it was scrub, scrub, scrub, spit. I was back to my old habit.

Why is it difficult to learn new habits? Because few of us are learning new habits. We're modifying old habits and old habits are exceedingly hard to change. Because you have all got a four-lane superhighway carved in your brain to do that habit (remember Tarzan Takes a Hike?).

You're modifying an already established, ingrained habit, which requires that the old habit gets pruned back over time and you have to start cutting a four-lane superhighway to the new habit. Your brain has to grow new dendrites and neurons to carry the messages for your "new" habit. That could take a lifetime. Don't be discouraged if after 28 days you haven't gotten rid of the old habit. You aren't fighting against your lack of willpower; you are fighting biology. Dendrites and neurons only grow so fast.

---

3. To clarify: I love my dentist. That other hygienist has long since transitioned out of my dentist's office. I love my current dental hygienist. She is remarkably good at her job. I am convinced she skipped the "Inducing Guilt and Shame" class.

The superhighway to the bad habit is so big and well used, it will take a long time for your brain to prune it back—for the jungle to grow over the roadbed.

M16s in Vietnam

How do you get there? How do you change your brain biology? Your success is a result of your habits. Mental rehearsal and **over-rehearsal** are the way. Only through over-rehearsal of a behavior can a person replace a bad habit (the Crocodile Swamp) with a nearly similar good habit (the Angel Falls).

Around 1999 or 2000, I spoke to a man who was a Vietnam combat veteran. He had volunteered for several combat tours in Vietnam. He had been out of the military for more than 25 years when I asked him "What was your service weapon?" He told me it was an M16. I asked him if he had handled the rifle since he left the military.

He said, "No. The last time I touched an M16 was in 1975 when I put it in the rack in the helicopter after they picked me up from my last patrol. I left it in the rack when I got off the chopper. I walked to my bunk, packed my stuff, and got ready to get the hell out of Vietnam."

Then I asked, "If I gave you an M16 today, do you think you could field-strip it?" Without hesitation he said "Yes, absolutely."

His wife chimed in at this point, "Oh no you couldn't." (At which point, I thought I'd have to start some marital therapy.) He looked back at her and replied, "Oh, yes I could." And I asked, "Why is that?"

He said, "I could do it with my eyes closed, hanging upside down, with mittens on. You see, the M16 was a new weapon platform at the time, and it was not super reliable. Not what you want in a rifle. The rifle used the gas created by the explosion in the cartridge to drive the bolt back to load another cartridge into the chamber. It was a pretty dirty mix of gas and smoke and tiny debris. All that debris would build up and clog the system. Add to that, it was so hot and humid and so dirty in Vietnam that it made it even worse. When you are in combat, you want to pull the trigger and have the rifle go 'bang'—not 'click.'

"We had to fieldstrip and clean our rifles several times each day. I liked to stay alive, so I'd fieldstrip it as many as a dozen times a day. I must have fieldstripped that rifle 3,000 to 10,000 times. I've done it so often, I could do it with my eyes closed, hanging upside down, and wearing mittens."

M16s to Piano Recitals

This illustrates the power of **over-learning**. If you are to be good at anything, you can't just learn it to the point that you get it right the first time, you have to over-learn it. When our children are learning to play the piano, we don't tell them to practice the piece until they get it right the first time. We tell them to practice it until they have it down cold.

There's no organization in the country that drills as much as the U.S. military. Why? They have their soldiers (or we could call them students) learn a skill, learn a motion, and then re-learn it and then learn it until it is not just learned, but it's over-learned. In that way, the student can repeat the behavior without thinking about it—it has become a habit.

The practice actually creates neural pathways in the brain so the behavior can be repeated without thought, even when under stress.

When people are under extreme stress, performance takes a dive. There are two ways to enhance performance:

1. Reduce environmental stress (not likely in a firefight)
2. Learn the act to the point of habit, so that it requires no thought (over-learning)

While you may have never been in a firefight, you are more likely to have had a piano recital. Your piano teacher made you over-learn your piece, because she knew that in the stress of the recital, your performance was likely to take a dive. She could have taught you deep breathing, centering strategies, or progressive muscle relaxation techniques to de-stress yourself for the recital. Or, she could have made you over-rehearse your music. Both can work, though it is easier and more reliable to have you over-rehearse. If you ever want to become excellent at anything, you must rehearse it over and over again until you can do it without thinking—so you can do it under stress, with your eyes closed, hanging upside down, wearing mittens.

Most of us don't want to focus on creating these kinds of habits. We'd like to do something adequately well and then quit. "That's good enough" is the refrain of the mediocre person. You can only become great at your task or your skill if you over-learn it and over-rehearse it. Most people don't want to commit to excellence. They don't want to commit to over-learning anything. Least of all, they don't want to commit to the constant training necessary to maintain excellence.

What makes one of the greatest golfers in the world? The golfer who is the first out on the practice tee and the last in at the end of the day. It's not because he's a better golfer than anyone (because at that level, they are all talented), it's because he practices more than anyone.

Natural skill will only take you so far, but over-learning your skill is what makes you great at what you do.

So how, you ask, can you get to the point of over-rehearsal? If you want to become excellent, you have to do the hard work of modifying your old habits. and here are three ways to do this: **novel reminders**, **irritating reminders**, and **stimulus control**.

1. Novel Reminders

Novel reminders take a stimulus from the environment over which you have no control, and associate that with a new pattern of thought or behavior.

How long is a Post-It Note effective?

In my experience, it's 48 hours. After two days, the Post-It Note becomes part of the background. Novel reminders are taking something that you have absolutely no control over and making that your reminder.

Here's how I learned this principle: When my first son was about to be born, the midwife told his mom that she needed to practice Kegel exercises. (For those of you who don't know what Kegel exercises are, I'm not going to tell you in detail. You can look them up for yourself. They help strengthen the pelvic floor muscles and make for healthier labor and delivery). The midwife gave us a pack of fluorescent stickers to put around the apartment to remind her to do her Kegels. Those stickers had the same effective life as a Post-It. After 48 hours, they just became bad home décor.

At our next visit the midwife said, "Okay, since that didn't work, how about you try this: Every time you are at a stoplight, you do 50 Kegels." This was genius. The midwife created a **novel reminder**. She took a stimulus over which we have no control—a red light—and associated it with a behavior we wanted—50 Kegels.

I've told this example to groups of women and dozens, if not hundreds have said their obstetrician or midwife recommended the same thing. Most also said that even 15, 20, or 30 years later, they still do their Kegels at the stoplight. They use a novel reminder to improve their physical health every day. But for our purposes, we are interested in using a novel reminder to change a thought habit. Can that work too? Yes!

I worked with a woman who was embittered because her husband was never home. He was always flying somewhere in an airplane to do his job. She had a little boy who was enamored with airplanes. So, my novel reminder assignment for her was this: "Every time your son points at an airplane, you need to look at the airplane and tell your son, 'That airplane is the kind Daddy flies in. He goes and earns money so we can buy the things we need.'"

She accepted the assignment but told me she thought it was a stupid idea. Every time she saw an airplane she told her son, "That's the kind of airplane Daddy flies in to earn money to buy the things we need." She came back in to see me six weeks later. She said that it seemed that in the last six weeks, her husband had become less of a jerk, and she was seeing more of his positive qualities. I told her I was really glad he had made those changes and their marriage had improved.

At the end of our meeting, I asked, "Did you do the airplane exercise?" She told me she had but wasn't sure why I assigned it. She never saw the connection between her changed thoughts about her husband and his being a jerk. Why had her attitude toward her husband changed? Because she had taken the novel stimulus of an airplane going overhead to remind herself to be grateful for her husband and his job.

Do you remember my pastor, Rev. Brosend? His story about the $20 bill and looking for change on the ground started me down the path of looking at pennies on the sidewalk differently. Those pennies became novel reminders that constantly direct me to think differently. This whole book is full of ways to tell yourself stories and find novel reminders to reshape your thinking and rewire your brain.

2. Irritating Reminders

Back to the dentist: My dentist and I have an open secret. Here it is: I hate to floss. I don't like wrapping dental floss around my fingers. It turns my fingers purple. It's slimy. It's hard to do. I just don't like it. So, he doesn't bother me about it, and I don't do it ("Inducing Guilt and Shame 101" may be required for dental hygienists but is an elective for dentists). But I can guarantee you that I will floss my teeth.

Here's how I do it: I buy those flossers with the dental floss string between two ends like a bow with a pointy end. Every time I want to floss my teeth, I just shove one of those flossers into my pocket. And why does that make me floss my teeth? That stupid thing sticks into my leg all day long and it irritates me to the point that I finally take it out to floss my teeth. That's how I can guarantee that I'll floss my teeth. (I recognize that some of you think this is gross, but it is my mouth.) If I reach into my pocket, I'm likely to get that pointy part jammed underneath my fingernail. That motivates me and **irritates** me to floss my teeth.

I also set reminders on my phone. You probably do the same thing on your phone. I have daily reminders set on my phone for how I want to think. Each day, I have a reminder of my life motto, my life goals (distilled into four words), and my word for the year. Each of those reminders keeps my head in the right space for a successful life. We soak in bad information all day long. The longer we soak in it, the more we take on that flavor. Much like barbequing—the longer the food soaks in the marinade, the more it takes on the flavor. I send out a "Daily Dose of Mental Marinade" that serves as an **irritating reminder** for people to soak in good stuff. It is a quote that I've chosen to help shape a person's thinking to be happier and more productive. If you'd like to get the Daily Dose of Mental Marinade, follow me on Twitter or Instagram @rogers2cents. If you'd like the email version, you can sign up at CompassConsultation.com or DrRogerHall.com.

3. Stimulus Control = Stupid Easy

Stimulus control is the most difficult way to create a habit but if well implemented, it is a nearly foolproof way of achieving behavior change.

It's about changing your environment so it's stupid easy to do the right thing. For example, when I was a kid I used to ride BMX bikes (down flights of stairs, off sweet jumps, and in skateboard parks). There was a kid who was a professional BMX racer. He was extremely good because he had very strong legs. I read about an interview with him where the interviewer asked him, "How was it that you got such huge legs?" and he said, "I got huge legs because I love to watch TV."

That didn't make any sense to me . . . until he explained.

He said "Yeah, I like to watch about four to five hours of TV a day and in my TV room, there's only one piece of furniture and that's an exercise bike. So if I want to watch TV, I've got to be pedaling." In other words, he set up his environment through stimulus control so that he couldn't help but exercise. By doing this, he made himself one of the great BMX racers of his era. It required planning and action (moving all the other furniture out of the room), but it created the result of making it stupid easy to exercise. Stimulus control is the hardest to set up but makes it the easiest to do the right thing.

If you want to modify an old habit, you can use one of these three methods to modify your old habit to change to a new habit. Success only comes to people who over-learn and over-rehearse the skills at which they want to be excellent.

Mental Monkey

The next time you are crossing the street or you see a photo of Winston Churchill, remember that habits, even good ones, if applied in the wrong situation, could get you killed.

The next time you are getting your teeth cleaned and you're getting lectured about your tooth brushing technique, remember that bad habits are really hard to change. They require that your brain regrow neurons to carry the new message. (Bonus: you can also remember that guilt and shame are lousy long-term motivators.)

Next time you are at a stoplight and wonder how to fill the time, do some Kegels, and remember that **novel reminders**, like these Mental Monkeys, are a good way to remind yourself to change your bad mental habits.

Next time you see an airplane flying overhead, think about what other things you can associate with that **novel reminder** to change your attitude.

Next time you stick your finger on something sharp in your pocket, think about how an **irritating reminder** can help you retrain your brain.

Next time you are barbequing, remember that the longer you soak in something, the more you take on its flavor. Marinate your thoughts in better things. And sign up for the Daily Dose of Mental Marinade.

Next time you set up a reminder on your phone, you're setting up an **irritating reminder**, which will eventually help you retrain your brain and your behavior.

Next time you see a BMX rider in the X-Games, think about how you can set up a **stimulus control** system so that you can't help but do the right thing to improve your life.

The Magic Act (Write This Down)

What **one** thing did I learn in this chapter that I can start applying now?

_____

_____

_____

_____

_____

What **bad habit** of thinking do I want to change after reading this chapter?

_____

_____

_____

_____

_____

_____

What thing in my life will be my "**Mental Monkey**" (my reminder) that will help me to change my thinking from what I learned in this chapter?

_____

_____

_____

_____

_____

_____

_____

_____

References

Colvin, G. (2008). *Talent Is Overrated: What Really Separates World-Class Performers From Everybody Else.* Portfolio Hardcover.

Coyle, D. (2009). *The Talent Code: Greatness Isn't Born. It's Grown. Here's How.* Bantam.

Clear, J. (2018). *Atomic Habits: An Easy & Proven Way to Build Good Habits & Break Bad Ones.* Avery.

Duhigg, C. (2012). *The Power of Habit: Why We Do What We Do in Life and Business.* Random House.

Etzioni, A. (1972, June 3). Human beings are not very easy to change after all. *Saturday Review,* 55.

Hardy, D. (2011). *The Compound Effect.* Vanguard Press.

Pressfield, S. (2003). *The War of Art: Break Through the Blocks and Win Your Inner Creative Battles.* Grand Central Publishing.

6

A MUSICIAN LIVING
RENT-FREE IN YOUR HEAD

Music and lyrics have a special kind of magic to help you change your thinking. They serve as very effective **novel reminders** to help you remember anything you associate with the music.

"'Stairway to Heaven' and 'Highway to Hell' indicate the amount of expected traffic."

—Unknown

The Slow Kid in Music Class

Music is a kind of magic to me. In grade school, I took violin lessons. I was not very good at violin, and there wasn't much future in being in a rock and roll band as a violinist, so I quit. Truth be told, I never really understood all the notes—half notes, quarter notes, and eighth notes, or bars, stanzas, and 4/4 versus 3/4 times. It was all a muddle to me. Some people can hear the difference and identify the musical pitch: "That is an A" or "That is a C-sharp." I cannot. I knew that I was going to have to choose a simpler instrument.

The selection of instruments you could play in a rock and roll band seemed pretty small. Bass was out. That was like the violin—four strings, no frets. If I couldn't figure it out on a small instrument, no way was I going to do any better on a bigger instrument, even without the bow. The guitar had six strings. Okay, that only increased the level of complexity. That was out. Piano? Eighty-eight keys, some white, some black, and pedals to do different things. Nope, that was out. Too complicated. What was left? Drums. Hey, I could succeed with that—no notes, and the drummers were cool. So, I took drum lessons.

At the end of nine months of public-school drum lessons, we had a band recital. Each of us in the class was assigned to a particular drum. Some got complicated snare drum parts. One guy got the steady one-and-three rhythm of the bass drum. That was for the slow kid, the one the teacher identified as unable to keep up with the rest of the band. That kid was me. And I screwed it up during the recital. The teacher had to keep giving me directions during the concert to keep the rhythm right. I was unable to follow his directions. On that day, I gave up my dreams of being a musician.

I moved up to junior high and met a whole set of kids who weren't in my grade school. One kid, Ben Ko, could whale on the piano like Jerry Lee Lewis. It was amazing. One day I asked him where he took his lessons. He hadn't. He couldn't read music. He learned to play by ear. In my mind, Ben was a magician. How was it possible to create this incredible music without a lesson, without reading music? How could someone listen to music and figure out how to play it? To someone like me, it was (and is) magic.

As a person with a tremendous love of music and no musical ability, I've had one small redeeming musical quality. I can usually think of a song for any situation I'm in.

Remember a job that ended badly? I start singing Elvis Costello's "Brilliant Mistake." Frustrated with a situation—Alice Cooper's "No More Mr. Nice Guy." Busy start to the week—the Bangles' "Manic Monday." If anyone mentions the capital of Turkey, it's the They Might Be Giants version of "Istanbul (Not Constantinople)." Smell a skunk on the highway, I start singing (badly) Louden Wainwright's "Dead Skunk." If you don't know it, it is worth a listen. You get the picture. Do you have a musician living rent-free in your head, too?

Bon Scott and a Church-Going Boy

I was a church-going boy, growing up. I don't think we ever missed a Sunday. Dad taught Sunday school. I knew all the hymns, usually three and four verses in. I knew the camp songs. I didn't sing loud (and still don't). Nobody wants to hear that.

I also listened to the radio. I woke every morning to my stereo clock radio. Somewhere around 6:30 a.m., in the glow of the green LEDs, the radio would spark on and wake me up with whatever song was playing. Invariably, that first song of the day would stick in my head for the rest of the day. One Monday morning in the 10th grade, four months after the release of the new AC/DC album, there I am, dialing in the combination of my Master Lock padlock singing that I'm on the highway to hell. I was immediately in a 15-year-old church boy's existential crisis. "Yesterday I was singing about heaven. Today I'm croaking like Bon Scott going to hell. Prickly heat crawled up my back to my neck. It was a sign. "Hell heck, am I going to be struck dead right here and go to hell?" I figured I had better take care to watch what music I listen to.[4] Bon Scott was living rent-free in my head.

Your Brain on Music (and Lyrics)

Back to some brain biology: the first thing you need to know is that the left side of your brain controls the right side of your body and vice versa. This isn't a perfect representation, but roughly speaking, it'll do. Now if you cup your hands over your ears, you'd be covering the temporal lobes of your brain. The temporal lobes of the brain are in charge of hearing, language (both spoken and written), rhythm, and music. Hearing noises (like a door creaking) is processed a little differently than sounds that make sense to us (like words), but those temporal lobes are involved in

---

4. For those of you who are convinced I am a religious prude, I am listening to AC/DC as I write this. For those of you who think I have bad taste in music, you may be right.

both. On the left side of your head above and a little in front of your left ear, there is a spot called Broca's Area that is in charge of producing words either through your mouth or through writing. There is a different area called Wernicke's Area (a little behind your left ear) that is in charge of understanding the written or spoken words.

There is no one particular spot in the brain that processes music—it's a host of related structures in some large areas of the brain—but mostly it happens in those earmuff spots called the temporal lobes. Studies of brain scans of people listening to music with and without lyrics suggest that those temporal lobes are working overtime in both cases. The sound going into your left ear starts a cascade of neurons shooting through the middle of your head to the right side of your brain. The same is true for the sound going into your right ear—the neurons shoot across the middle of your brain to the left temporal lobe.

When you are listening to music with lyrics, the left side of your head is working a little bit harder. It seems that the language processing centers on the left side get engaged when you are listening to music with lyrics. It also seems that the right temporal lobe is associated with the ability to process rhythm. In fact, when people listen to music that is emotional to them, the right temporal lobe lights up (when compared to silence and when listening to music that isn't emotional to them).

Some studies suggest that the more familiar the song, the more likely some deep limbic structures like the amygdala and putamen will light up as well—these are likely related to the emotions the music evokes, and so are some image retrieval spots (like you are remembering an image from a memory).

In other words, music lights up all kinds of places crisscrossing all over both sides of your brain, from the front to the back of your ears, and into the deep structures of your brain.

Music (especially with lyrics) evokes memories, images, and emotions, and integrates many brain activities.

In my case and in Bon Scott's, some of the guilt and fear centers in my limbic system were activated, too.

Schoolhouse Rock

I dare you. I double-dare you to try to say the alphabet without singing the alphabet song. (I've practiced at home to see if I can.) It is harder than you might think. Why is that? Because when music is involved, words are easier to recall. In the 1970s and 1980s (and then revived briefly in the 1990s) there were Saturday morning cartoons called *Schoolhouse Rock* that featured a lesson (on language, math, science, or civics) put to a song. I'll wager that people who saw those cartoons can still sing along to "Conjunction Junction, what's your function?" or "I'm Just a Bill." It was genius! Teach kids stuff to a song and it will never leave their minds. You can look up the videos online and they will get stuck in your head as well.

Your brain is better at remembering stuff if it is put to a tune or rhythm. If we give undergraduates a list of words to memorize, we can improve their memory for the words if we put the words to a tune or a rhythm. The music and rhythm seem to "chunk" the words into meaningful ways, so they are easier to remember.

If the stream of consciousness in your head is full of unproductive thoughts, you can replace them with more productive ones. If you put the more productive thoughts to a tune, they are easier to recall. When you hear the song out in the wild (at the grocery store, a restaurant, or on your streaming mix of songs), it becomes a **novel reminder** to think the more productive thought. (Remember chapter 5? Novel reminders are things you have no control over that remind you of a way to think.) Songs are the *perfect* novel reminder. You never know when they are coming and they can put you in a better state of mind, lasso your errant thoughts, and make you happier.

You already have dozens of musicians living rent-free in your head. Which ones are you giving more space? If your stream of consciousness is flowing full of trash, how can you replace that trash with something better? Start finding songs to change your thinking! Your taste in music doesn't have to be like mine, but what you are listening to is changing your brain—for good or for ill. Sure, I still listen to AC/DC, but when I want to get my mind in shape, I put different tunes on my playlist.

My Playlist

You don't have to like my music, but these songs (music and lyrics) put me in the right state of mind.

"Are You Gonna Go My Way?" – Lenny Kravitz (If I ever had "walk on" music, I would want it to be Lenny's anthem. No question.)

"Holding On to You" – Twenty One Pilots (These lyrics are worth a read. They come as close to what I'm trying to do here as any other song on the list: putting destructive thoughts on a leash and replacing them with more productive ones. You can be in control of your mind.)

"Mr. Blue Sky" – Electric Light Orchestra

"Meant to Live" – Switchfoot

"(What's So Funny 'Bout) Peace, Love and Understanding" – Elvis Costello and the Attractions (written by Nick Lowe)

"Hey Ya!" – Outkast (Perhaps not the best lyrics, but who doesn't want to shake it like a Polaroid picture?)

"Roll Over Beethoven" – Chuck Berry (or Electric Light Orchestra)

"Good Times Roll" – The Cars

"Freedom of Choice" – Devo

"Pork and Beans" – Weezer

"When You Were Young" – The Killers

"Sweet Child O' Mine" – Guns N' Roses

"What a Wonderful World" – Louis Armstrong (Joey Ramone's cover is good in a different way.)

"Wonderful Tonight" – Eric Clapton

"When Will I Ever Learn to Live in God" – Van Morrison (Phil Keaggy's cover is also awesome.)

"Too Dumb for New York City, Too Ugly for L.A." – Waylon Jennings

"Amazing Grace" – Johnny Cash

"Stressed Out" – Twenty One Pilots

"Bless the Broken Road" – The Nitty Gritty Dirt Band

"Then" – Brad Paisley

"In the Mood" – Glenn Miller (This is an example of a song with no lyrics that *everyone* knows and usually makes them happy, regardless of their taste in music.)

"Walking on Sunshine" – Katrina and the Waves

"Me and Bobby McGee" – Janis Joplin (I am partial to Kris Kristofferson's take on his own song.)

"Everything Works If You Let It" – Cheap Trick

"That's Amore" – Dean Martin

"I Want to Be Like You" – Louie Prima (from the Jungle Book cartoon movie)

"You'll Never Walk Alone" – Elvis Presley

"Somewhere Over the Rainbow" – Israel IZ Kamakawiwo'ole

"Just Wanna See His Face" – Blind Boys of Alabama (a version of the Rolling Stones riff)

"Old Me Better" – Keb' Mo' (I know, I know, the lyrics are in almost direct opposition of this whole book, but the song makes me laugh, and I think it will make you laugh too.)

"We Don't Need It" – Keb' Mo' (This one will make you cry, in a good way.)

"William Blake" – Daniel Amos

"A Blessing in Disguise" – The Lost Dogs (I think I've listened to this song a thousand times. It has helped me in difficult times in my life. Thanks guys.)

If you want to listen to all the music referenced in this book, you can visit the DrRogerHall channel on YouTube. Here is the link: https://www.youtube.com/user/DrRogerHall. Navigate to the playlists, and you'll find the DIY Brain playlist.

What is in your playlist? The songs may represent your current state of mind. There are times for sad songs. That is okay, but do you want to stay there? If you're at the Crocodile Swamp in your mind, do you want to stay there, listening to "Girlfriend in a Coma"? It probably makes you feel lousy. If you're reading this book, it suggests you don't want to stay at the Crocodile Swamp. By changing your playlist, you can change the destination of your mind and end up at the Angel Waterfall.

Mental Monkey

Next time you hear yourself singing a tune, ask yourself: What are the lyrics saying?

Next time you are listening to your streaming service, monitor how you feel with the music.

Next time you are at a concert, ask yourself, "Does this music help my mindset or hurt it?"

Next time you're bouncing around between stations on your car radio, ask yourself, "Is this good for my head?"

The Magic Act (Write This Down)

What song will I use as a **novel reminder** to retrain my brain?

_____

_____

_____

_____

What should I put on my own *DIY Brain* Playlist (start writing here)? How and when can I put it in heavy rotation?

_____

_____

_____

_____

What one thing did I learn in this chapter that I can start applying now?

_____

_____

_____

_____

_____

What **bad habit** of thinking do I want to change after reading this chapter?

_____

_____

_____

_____

_____

What thing in my life will be my "**Mental Monkey**" (my reminder) that will help me to change my thinking from what I learned in this chapter?

_____

_____

_____

_____

References

Alfredson, B.B., Risberg, J., Hagberg, B. & Gustafson, L. (2004). Right temporal lobe activation when listening to emotionally significant music. *Applied Neuropsychology, 11*(3), 161-166.

Alluri, V., Toiviainen, P., Lund, T.E., Wallentin, M., Vuust, P., Nandi, A. K., Nandi, A.K. & Brattico, E. (2013). From Vivaldi to Beatles and back: predicting lateralized brain responses to music. *Neuroimage, 83*, 627-636.

Boone, K.B. & Rausch, R. (1989). Seashore Rhythm Test performance in patients with unilateral temporal lobe damage. *Journal of Clinical Psychology, 45*(4), 614-618.

Brattico, E., Alluri, V., Bogert, B., Jacobsen, T., Vartiainen, N., Nieminen, S.K. & Tervaniemi, M. (2011). A functional MRI study of happy and sad emotions in music with and without lyrics. *Frontiers in Psychology, 2*, 308.

Purnell-Webb, P. & Speelman, C.P. (2008). Effects of music on memory for text. *Perceptual and Motor Skills, 106*(3), 927-957.

Sammler, D., Baird, A., Valabrègue, R., Clément, S., Dupont, S., Belin, P. & Samson, S. (2010). The relationship of lyrics and tunes in the processing of unfamiliar songs: a functional magnetic resonance adaptation study. *Journal of Neuroscience, 30*(10), 3572-3578.

Satoh, M., Takeda, K., Nagata, K., Shimosegawa, E. & Kuzuhara, S. (2006). Positron-emission tomography of brain regions activated by recognition of familiar music. *American Journal of Neuroradiology, 27*(5), 1101-1106.

⑦

MY PAL AL

A description of one type of cognitive therapy and the story of why it really, really works. It's (almost) as easy as the ABCs.

Lonely in a Crowd

In my first quarter of graduate school, I spent every week sitting in Lyle Schmidt's Introduction to Counseling course with a group of academically competitive students. Everyone in the class was already an excellent student. They had come from various parts of the country. Each had impressive grades and test scores. It was a time in school when we simultaneously wanted to fit in and stand out, and even though we barely knew each other, we did know that we were stuck together for the next few years. It was in this context that Dr. Schmidt wheeled out the 24-inch console TV on an A/V cart containing a VCR the size of a small washing machine. He pushed the button and plopped in his tape of Everett Shostrom's *The Gloria Films*.

Everett Shostrom was not a movie producer but a well-known psychotherapist and psychologist who recognized the power of color movie film to tell a story, and in 1965 he used the then-new technology to demonstrate three different psychotherapies with the same real client named Gloria. In fact, at the time of the filming, Gloria was actually in therapy with Shostrom, and unbeknownst to the viewers, she had already been in therapy with two of the three world-renowned psychologists profiled in the film: Carl Rogers, Fritz Perls, and Albert Ellis.

Gloria's first session was with Carl Rogers, whose so-called client-centered psychotherapy was nondirective and pleasant. Rogers acted like a very pleasant man and asked Gloria lots of questions about how she felt. In fact, the therapy shown greatly resembled a conversation with the cardigan-clad Fred Rogers of *Mr. Rogers' Neighborhood* but without any advice.

Next, Gloria was shown in a session with Fritz Perls, who used an approach that exaggerated things she said and insisted that she act out some awkward physical behaviors. It is a little like watching a bad kid poke an animal with a stick until the animal strikes back. With his thick German accent, his bow tie, and his nearly constant smoking, Perls called her a phony, then pestered her about kicking her foot, waving her hands, pointing her finger at him, exaggerating her disgusted face, and ended up initiating an elaborate game of verbal tennis.

Gloria's final session was with Albert Ellis, a prototypical New Yorker with a nasal voice who came across as pushy and abrasive. He confronted Gloria's "irrational" thoughts and debated with her about the irrationality of her thoughts. These are central tenets of his rational-emotive therapy (later called rational-emotive behavior therapy, or REBT). At moments, he went off on brief rants, and throughout the session he was never very sensitive or supportive. By all appearances, he was not a very nice man.

In the end of the film, when Gloria is asked to choose which of the three sessions she felt was the most effective, she chose the sparring with Fritz Perls.

Turning off the VCR, Dr. Schmidt asked us, by a show of hands, who *we* thought was the most effective.

"How about Carl Rogers?" About half the class raised their hands.

"How about Fritz Perls?" Again, about half of the class raised their hands.

"Anyone think Albert Ellis did the best job?" One lonely hand. Mine.

My classmates slowly turned toward me, staring in disbelief. Some rolled their eyes. I heard someone mutter, "You've got to be kidding me." As I saw it, he was the only one who took seriously the problem she came in with and took steps to help her solve it. Was he annoying? Sure, but it appears he actually listened and had a system to help her.

From that day forward, in our graduate program, Albert Ellis was known as "my pal Al." My classmates teased me, but research has vindicated my choice. Ellis's Rational Emotive Behavior Therapy has been shown to be the only one of the three types of therapy to be more effective than a placebo. In other words, if you worked with Rogers or Perls, you would have had as much improvement as talking to a goldfish (so long as you thought the goldfish could help you). Ellis's approach is actually effective.

The Alphabet Can Help You Keep Your Sanity

Even though Ellis is not really my pal, I met him once and saw him speak a couple of times. And he was in person exactly how I remembered him from the film—salty, grumbling, and more inclined to grouse than coddle. And despite the fact that you'd probably never want to invite him to your kid's birthday party, before his death he was probably one of the last living greats among professional psychotherapists.

One of the most challenging parts about changing our behavior is remembering to do it, or remembering that we even *want* to do it. The brilliance of Ellis's theory is that it used the alphabet as a mnemonic to help us remember how to change our thinking. His theory fundamentally changed psychotherapy—and he didn't even go all the way through the alphabet. I've tweaked Ellis's model a little bit, but this is basically his theory.

The first step is to write the first five letters (notice there are four D's and two E's), one per line, on a sheet of paper, going from top to bottom, like so:

A

B

C

D

D

D

D

E

E

Grandma's Dead

The *A* in Ellis's ABC Model stands for **A̲dversity** (or sometimes more accurately, the **A̲ctivating Event**). When people come to adversity in life, they can name it. They put a stake in it and make it a landmark for life. Let's say for our example that my grandmother died. (Both of my grandmothers have already passed away, and none of what I'm about to say about my grandmothers is true; it's just for the purposes of our discussion here.) So, in our example, the adversity is that Grandma dies. Most people think that the adversity causes the **C̲onsequence**. (You guessed it: *C* stands for consequence, usually an emotional consequence. In psychotherapy, this is the consequence that is distressing to you—the thing you want to change.) In our example, the emotional consequence of my grandmother's death is that I feel sad or I feel bad.

(If you can't name an emotion, I tell people to start with the list of emotions from Dr. Seuss's *One Fish, Two Fish, Red Fish, Blue Fish:* "Sad and glad and bad? I do not know. Go ask your Dad." So simple yet genius.)

Thoughts on Grandma

Most people think that my grandmother dying *causes* this emotional reaction; it's the reason *why* I feel bad or sad. But that's not true. The event *does not* cause the consequence.

The event creates a **Belief**—the thought I have about the event. If my grandmother dies, and I *believe* that I'll miss her because I loved her, the consequence is that I'll be sad. Broken down, it looks like this:

- **Adversity** is my grandmother's death.
- **Belief** is that I'll miss her (an accurate belief, which we'll get into in a moment).
- **Consequence** is that I'll be sad.

Now, my grandmother's death doesn't *necessarily* make me sad. The thing that makes me sad is my **belief** about my grandmother's death. Watch what happens when we change the belief to "Oh good, the old bird's dead, now I get the money!" The activating event of my grandmother's death creates a different belief (it isn't an adversity this time because it isn't bad). So, if I believe "The old bird's dead and now I get the money," then my emotional consequence changes to "I'm glad." I'm a happy camper because I get all the cash.

Most people don't come to me and say, "Boy, I have this pleasant belief I'd like to talk to you about," mostly because accurate and pleasant beliefs lead to positive emotional consequences, which are the things people talk about with their friends over beers, not with psychologists like me.

What people tend to share with their psychologists are inaccurate or problematic beliefs, which lead to unpleasant emotions that they'd like to sort out (which is okay, because that's my job—talking with people about their wrong beliefs or their unpleasant emotions).

Scarlett O'Hara Makes You Sick

Now, when you have an incorrect or unproductive belief, there are four ways to **deal** with it. The first is **Denial** (D_1). This is "Scarlett O'Hara" denial—"I'll think about it . . . tomorrow." If you haven't seen the movie *Gone with the Wind*, Scarlett O'Hara's method for solving problems was to *not* think about them. In the midst of the burning of Atlanta in the Civil War, her solution was to tell herself, "I'll think about it tomorrow," and go to bed. Scarlett O'Hara denial can be summed up in three words: **pretend**

and forget. If a bad thing occurs, you pretend it didn't happen and you forget about it. You just put it out of your mind.

As for me, I can't do denial—I don't know *how* to do denial—but a lot of people can. They just say "I just won't think about it. That's an unpleasant thought. I don't do unpleasant thoughts, so I won't think about it." And they're done. So what does denial look like in practice? Let's go back to the example of my grandmother.

Imagine that, when a close friend offers me condolences on my grandmother's death, I respond, "She's not dead. I don't know why you'd say that. She's a little under the weather, but tomorrow, she'll be as right as rain." How unhinged does that sound? I can't do that. Maybe you can't either, but some people can.

In my experience, I routinely find that people who use denial tend to have stress-related physical problems. These are illnesses like irritable bowel syndrome, ulcerative colitis, migraine headaches, high blood pressure, high cholesterol, and adrenal problems, among a host of others. Stress-related illnesses are caused, exacerbated, or extended because of psychological distress.

These somatic (physical) ailments arise, get worse, or stay around longer because the conscious brain is not thinking about the distressing event, the adversity. The person's conscious brain is not even thinking about the wrong belief or the unproductive belief. In fact, they are not even aware of the emotional consequence. But even though their conscious brain isn't thinking about A, B or C, their emotional brain, the limbic system, is still activated. In fact, the limbic system is going a mile a minute, sending a cascade of signals to their pituitary, thyroid, and adrenal glands, which then flood the body with stress chemicals. When too many of these chemicals are running around the bloodstream, they cause stress-related illnesses or somatic problems. The body is literally preparing to fight or run away from some kind of danger—a danger that is unresolved and not even being addressed.

People who use denial don't even realize that their body is perpetually activating the fight-or-flight response, but it is, and when the body systems that are activated during this response wear out, people develop a host of stress-related, somatic illnesses. This is *not* hypochondriasis. These are real illnesses that are caused by emotional distress.

Denial tends to create somatic problems. As a psychologist, I see people with all kinds of physical problems who have a habit of putting their unpleasant emotions and beliefs out of their mind. Denial is a *negative short-term* and a *negative long-term* solution to these distressing beliefs. In short, thinking like Scarlett O'Hara makes you sick.

Babies, Booze, and Bad Television

The second way people deal with unpleasant emotions is called **Distraction** (D_2). It's very similar to denial except that the person uses an outside activity to distract him or her from the incorrect or unproductive belief. This is a *positive short-term*, *negative long-term* solution.

I'm really, really good at distraction and I'll bet you are, too. In the example of my grandmother dying, if I say, "I feel sad because my grandmother died because I'm going to miss her," that's a true statement. We don't want to argue against that. But once I add to that by saying, "I'm just so tired of feeling sad. I want to go to the movies so I don't have to feel sad for two hours," then I'm using a movie as a short-term distraction, which is perfectly acceptable.

If after a year I'm still in the movie theater, however, then it becomes destructive.

People use all sorts of things to distract themselves from thoughts that cause emotional distress. They use sex. They use drugs. They use alcohol. They become overinvolved in their work. They become overinvolved in their kids. They distract themselves with anything that will keep them from thinking about the difficulty or adversity in their life. None of this is bad in the *short run*. It's only destructive in the *long run*. Consider sex, for example. After the World Trade Center attack on September 11, nine months later, lots and lots of babies were born. Why is that? Because in the distress of that tragic event, people turned to one another and had sex. This was a perfectly acceptable response. It would only become a problem if after a year, people were doing nothing but having sex or being involved with sex in a destructive way.

Let's look at alcohol. Sometimes people drink alcohol to "take the edge off." Doing this occasionally and for a short term does not indicate a problem. If someone finds themselves virtually living in the bar and starts having problems because of alcohol, then their short-term distraction has become an unhealthy long-term solution. Alcohol is a decent short-term solution but a lousy long-term solution.

Distraction is the American way of life and our solution to almost every problem. At the very least, we typically entertain ourselves to keep from thinking about our problems. We are an entertainment-saturated and media-centered society.

Because we use entertainment all the time, we are challenged by the still-ness required for falling asleep and have a great deal of difficulty with the silence that comes when lying in bed looking at the ceiling. Why? Because nothing is *happening*. Unable or unwilling to confront the 15 minutes of mental quiet required to fall asleep, people often turn on the television in their bedrooms and set the sleep timer. In bed, they use the TV, phone, or tablet as a distraction until they fall asleep, filling their head with noise so they can avoid thinking about the distressing aspects of their life.

Similarly, some people may not have trouble falling asleep initially but are plagued by waking up in the middle of the night, unable to go back to sleep because a flood of distressing beliefs is keeping us awake. A common response is to turn on the television (or the cellphone or laptop) for some late-night entertainment, infomercials, binge-watching, or 4 a.m. surfing and shopping.

They don't find a pad of paper to write down all the distressing beliefs they have and list what they are distressed about. They never, ever examine what is troubling in their lives. Even though people use entertainment in our society as a distraction, there is nothing inherently wrong with entertainment. What *is* wrong is using entertainment as a long-term means of distracting yourself from examining all of your incorrect or unproductive thoughts. If I am constantly drinking or using media to alleviate my symptoms, I never get about the business of *solving* my problems. The problems stick around and I wonder why I never feel any better.

Like those who use denial, long-term distraction has the same bodily consequences. Your brain and body are in constant fight-or-flight mode. In addition to suffering from the somatic illnesses, people who use distraction become what I call "conversation hoppers." In my experience, I have found that people who use distraction as their primary way of dealing with distressing beliefs are unable to stay on any topic of conversation for any length of time. In psychological terms, this is called **tangential conversation**—the person is following rabbit trails of conversation, going all over the place and never stopping to linger on any topic.

A related concept is called **circumstantial speech**, which is a kind of superficial speech in which people skim across the surface of a conversation but never go into any depth. In both tangential conversation and circumstantial speech, people dart like hummingbirds from topic to topic, never staying on any one for any length of time and never diving deeply into any. I find that when I work with someone distracted in this way, they squirm to no end in a perpetual attempt to keep from thinking about what we're talking about.

Lying to Myself

D_1 is denial, D_2 is distraction, and D_3 is **self-<u>D</u>eception**. Self-deception is telling yourself pleasant—or unpleasant—little lies. This is also known as **rationalization**. In his book, *17 Lies That Are Holding You Back and the Truth That Will Set You Free*, Steve Chandler wrote, "To rationalize is to tell yourself rational lies."

My favorite example of rationalization can be found in people who buy classic convertible MGs or Triumphs—sleek and stylish British cars that came out in the 1960s and '70s. As good as they look, mechanically they are complete hunks of junk. Nonetheless, they garnered quite a following, and new owners joined MG car clubs soon after buying one. Members gathered in shabby garages in loose circles of metal folding chairs for meetings, the agendas of which consisted mostly of telling each other what a great idea it was to buy these stupid cars. Car owners were often heard saying, "Oh, she's a beauty out on the road. Boy, you put the top down on a spring weekend and drive around. It's so much fun."

What these MG owners were never heard saying was that after driving once around the block, they had to take the head gasket out and replace it, which would take up three whole weekends. So, for the one weekend you get to drive the car, you have to spend three weekends putting it back together. What you did hear at these meetings were whoppers like, "Oh, I always like a little grease on my hands. It's fun for me to troubleshoot electrical problems. I like the mental challenge." And my personal favorite, told to me by an actual classic MG owner, has always been this doozy: "Part of the excitement of driving an MG is you never know where you're going to break down." Wow. Really?

That is a prime example of rationalization, or telling yourself a pleasant little lie. People do this all the time. It's the foundation of buyer's remorse. Everyone's regretted a purchase decision at some point. It could have been a snack, a pair of shoes, an electronic device, a car, or even a house. Perhaps you weren't really hungry, you didn't really need them, it didn't turn out the way you wanted, or you couldn't return it. So, you made the best of it and told yourself pleasant little lies to make yourself feel like it was a good decision. Rather than 'fess up and say, "Boy, I made a mistake," you tell yourself some pleasant little story about what you've done.

On the surface, self-deception may seem harmless, but it has a dark side: Once you make a bad decision and lie to yourself about it, you are far more likely to double down on your bad decision and stick with it. Take those classic MG owners, for example. Those MGs had two consistent problems: electrical shorts and leaking oil. Occasionally, those two problems occurred simultaneously and caused flames to shoot out of the air vents into the car, as the electrical short lit the oil leak on fire. I'm not making this up. Former classic MG owners have confessed seeing this phenomenon to me.

What do you think a completely self-deceived MG owner would do? Let's say you buy an old restored MG, join the MG car club, and become president of your local chapter. Then the oil leak and electrical short problem get together and your car burns to the ground. Do you concede and say, "I should have never bought that hunk of crap."? No. You double down and buy another classic MG.

I told this story to a group of workshop attendees once, and at the break, a man came up to me and said, "You know that thing you were talking about? That's me."

"Which thing?" I asked.

"The MG thing."

I winced, thinking he was going to take a swing at me. Waiting to be punched, I said, "Oh, I'm really sorry!"

He replied, "No, you're absolutely right. I'm the president of the local MG car club."

I winced again.

He continued, "It's like a disease. I own 30."

I told him his problem was far beyond my skill level.

Classic MG car owners and other rationalizers double down on their bad decisions and make even *worse* decisions!

How do I know? Because when I tell other classic MG owners about the guy with 30 MGs, they reply (almost in unison), "Well, most of those are probably for parts."

The Best Lies Are Mostly True

You can see how pleasant little lies will get you into trouble, but so will the unpleasant little lies. And the best, most believable lies are mostly true. We can easily spot this lie about my grandmother: "I never loved her. She smelled funny." That is an obvious unpleasant lie. The much more damaging lie is this: "I miss Grandma [true], and I don't think I can ever get over this [pernicious little lie that will stick in the back of your head and roll around for years]." This lie is mostly true, and that's why it is the most dangerous! The difference between a very believable lie and the truth is the quality of the **Evidence** (the first E in our formula).

Talking to Yourself

D_4, the final D, is **Disputation**, or arguing with yourself. The only difference between disputation and deception is that disputation is based on the truth, on **Evidence** (E_1). You need to gather evidence *against* your wrong belief. Remember, it is hard to distinguish truth from lies because the best lies are mostly true. Now if your belief is wrong, you shouldn't believe it. If your belief is correct, you should believe it. This last one, disputation, is often the hardest to do by yourself. At this point, you may want to bring in a trusted friend, advisor, spiritual guide, or competent psychotherapist to help you figure out how to argue with yourself—to determine if your beliefs are accurate or inaccurate.

For example, if I'm sad because my grandmother died, that's a true belief, the consequence of which is that I'm sad. Do I need to dispute this idea? No, I don't need to dispute this idea at all because it's an accurate belief. However, if my grandmother died and I believe that I'll never be happy again (deception) and therefore I'm sad, then I need to argue (dispute) with myself. I need to dispute with myself based on evidence: I observe people throughout my life whose loved ones died and they go on to live happy, productive lives. I tell myself grief is a normal part of the life process. While it hurts for a while, longer than any of us want, most people go on to be happy again.

Trying to escape grief won't get us what we want. If we accept it, we experience it. And once we've experienced it, then we can move on to a happy life. Based on that piece of evidence, all we have to do is tell ourselves the truth. The truth is I'm sad because my grandmother died. This sadness won't last forever. The grief I'm experiencing is normal and will eventually recede into the background, at which point I'll go back to leading a happy life. Very often the self-deception is so pervasive, we need to rehearse our disputation based on evidence over and over and over again.

Fancy Greek Philosophy

So the first E is evidence. We've seen that. E_2, the final E, is to lead an **Examined life**, which, according to the ancient Greek philosopher Socrates, is the only one worth living. If you examine your beliefs, tell yourself the truth, argue against the wrong beliefs, don't deceive yourself, don't overly distract yourself with entertainment and idle activities, and don't deny the difficulties in your life, you will lead a fulfilling, constructive life.

It's only when you regularly and decidedly practice arguing with yourself about your wrong ideas that you can have an examined, productive life.

Now you try. Fill out the ABCs of a problem plaguing you. Fill in the **Adversity**, the **Consequence** of that adversity, and identify the **Beliefs** that drive the consequence. Then **Dispute** those deceptive beliefs with **Evidence**.

A =

DIY BRAIN

B =

C =

D =

E =

Mental Monkey

The next time you sing or hear the alphabet song, remind yourself that you can change your problematic thinking with the first five of those letters.

Next time you hear the word *rationalize,* remind yourself of what best-selling author Steve Chandler said: rationalize means "rational lies."

Next time you read Dr. Seuss's *One Fish, Two Fish, Red Fish, Blue Fish* to your kids, remember that you can identify the negative emotional consequences of your problematic thoughts.

Whenever you hear someone make a reference to *Gone with the Wind,* remember that when Scarlett O'Hara says, "I'll think about it tomorrow," she's using denial. And denial is a bad short-term *and* bad long-term solution to unproductive beliefs.

When after a long day (or week) at work, you have a drink, go out to the movies, or surf the internet until late into the night, remind yourself that these distractions are great short-term but lousy long-term solutions.

When you see a classic MG or Triumph on the road (not likely) or in a movie, remind yourself that we lie to ourselves all the time. What lies are you telling yourself?

Next time you hear a nasally New Yorker like Albert Ellis, remind yourself that you can change your emotions or mood by changing the way you think.

The Magic Act (Write This Down)

What **one** thing did I learn in this chapter that I can start applying now?

_____

_____

_____

_____

_____

_____

_____

_____

What **bad habit** of thinking do I want to change after reading this chapter?

_____

_____

_____

_____

_____

_____

_____

_____

What thing in my life will be my "**Mental Monkey**" (my reminder) that will help me to change my thinking from what I learned in this chapter?

_____

_____

_____

_____

_____

_____

_____

_____

_____

_____

What reminders have I posted lately to remind myself to stay on the correct path?

_____

_____

_____

_____

_____

_____

_____

_____

_____

References

Ellis, A. (1991). The revised ABCs of rational-emotive therapy (RET). *Journal of Rational-Emotive and Cognitive-Behavior Therapy*, *9*(3), 139-172.

Seligman, M.E., Ph.D. (2009). *What You Can Change . . . and What You Can't*: The Complete Guide to Successful Self-Improvement. *Learning to Accept Who You Are.* Vintage.

SLUG BUG

How a teenage game will help you understand why it seems that bad things happen to you all the time. Plus stories about how the concepts of *priming* and the *availability heuristic* lead to erroneous thoughts.

A Tale of Two Beetle Owners

As a graduate student, I drove a Volkswagen (VW) Beetle. This was a 1977 version—one of the old ones. It was white with black seats and black carpet and a black steering wheel. It sputtered and putted up to about 55 miles per hour until the whole body shook. I didn't dare go much faster. One time, the accelerator cable snapped, and the car glided to the side of the highway. I was told later that I could have used my shoestring to make the repair. And I was on a shoestring budget at the time.

Things changed with the last generation of Beetles. They were hot little cars. The old ones were hot, but for entirely different reasons—no air conditioning in the summer and temperamental heaters in the winter. I've talked to dozens of people who owned the old Beetles. There are two kinds of stories these people tell.

Beetle owners either say, "The great thing about Beetles was that anyone could fix them with the tools you had lying around the house. I remember replacing the engine with a bungee cord and a screwdriver one Saturday afternoon. It was so much fun." (A 97-pound woman always tells this story.) "Oh, I wish I had never gotten rid of that car. It was so much fun to drive. I loved it."

Or they say, "I was nearly killed in a VW Beetle."

Ask around. I guarantee those are the only two stories you'll hear about the old VW Beetles. Mine is of the second variety: I was nearly killed in that VW.

Maybe, if you are the observant sort, you have already figured out that little car and I were not best friends. I drove it nearly every day for four years. In that time, I learned a lot about how to fix the accelerator cable with a shoestring, how to scrape ice from the inside of the windshield while I was driving, and how to walk long distances.

I also learned about mental errors like this one: "This car is bad luck and trouble." Except for the fact that I was nearly being killed in that VW on a daily basis, that statement is generally a mental error. Despite my hate-hate relationship with that VW, it was responsible for me figuring out two mental errors we make related to how we encode and retrieve memories of events.

The first error is related to how the brain encodes, or records, events. This mental shortcut that is sometimes erroneous is called **priming** (and compared to the neuropsychological vocabulary we had a few chapters ago, is easy to pronounce). Priming describes how *the context of an event shapes how you encode the event*. It is typically an unconscious action. You don't really think about how you record the event in your brain, you just do it. "And," you ask, "what does this have to do with VW Beetles?"

I'm so glad you asked.

Did you ever play Slug Bug? (The alternate, less-preferred name is Punch Buggy). Here are the rules: As you drive along the road, the first person who sees a VW Beetle yells "Slug Bug!" in a loud voice, which confers the divine right to punch the other person in the car as hard as they can.

That's it. That's the game. Whee! Wasn't that fun?

Picture if you will, me driving my VW on a wintry February day, scraping the ice off the inside of the windshield. I take my glove off and use the warmth of my hand to defrost a spot on the windshield (true story). I look through the eight-square-inch clear spot in the ice, only to see the adolescent male passenger of an oncoming Ford F-250 pickup truck mouthing the words "Slug Bug." This occurs simultaneously as I see him draw back his right arm, fist clenched, only to release it in a direct pile-driving motion to clobber the driver in the right arm. Then imagine (in slow motion) the driver (hands at ten and two) flinching as he awaits the oncoming fist, then buckling as his shoulder takes the shot. Use your powers of deduction and knowledge of physics to figure out what happens to his steering at this moment.

While you do this, did I mention I was nearly killed in that VW?

Yes, the driver invariably pulls left of center toward me, the guy in the rickety VW. Did I mention the steering was loose and the brakes were marginal? Yes, I was nearly killed in that VW. More than once.

Even though I can't prove this, I am sure this game, Slug Bug, was great for VW Beetle sales. Why? Because of priming. Every time an adolescent boy saw a VW Beetle, his pulse quickened, because he was primed to watch out for them. He had been classically conditioned to have an increased heart rate in preparation for a mighty wallop to the arm. This priming has a predictable effect. He was always prepared or primed to see Beetles. They were on the top of his mind.

Having a thought on the top of your mind changes the way you encode information about the world.

The Junk Drawer in Your Kitchen

Do you have a junk drawer in your kitchen? If you are mentally healthy, of course you do. (Those of you without junk drawers in your kitchen, please do not write me nasty notes. Go immediately to a mental health professional for assistance.) You know what it looks like. It is full of all the stuff that has no better place to go. In it, you throw the scissors, the flashlight, pizza coupons, a sheet of stamps, pens, rubber bands, paper clips, and all the rest of the detritus of household life.

So, what is on the top of your junk drawer?

The answer varies, depending on what you have *most frequently or recently used*. On top is whatever you put in and take out of the junk drawer often, or the last thing you tossed in there. What is in the back? You have no idea. You haven't been to the back of your junk drawer since you moved into the place.

Your memory is like your junk drawer. Whatever thought or memories are most frequently or recently accessed are on the top of your mind. Priming is one of the processes that puts it there.

Back to VW Beetles

The junk-drawer effect helps us understand how the game of Slug Bug contributes to our memory of the VW Beetle. It's responsible in part for our impression that VW Beetles are *everywhere* and that *everyone* drives one. When it comes to recalling how many VW Beetles are on the road, every adolescent kid who has ever played Slug Bug would probably say there were tons of them. Why? Because their autonomic nervous system took a jolt of adrenaline every time they saw one. This made it easier to recall. They have been primed to see VW Beetles. Beetles were on the top of their memory junk drawer.

When I drove my VW, long past their heyday, I saw them everywhere, but really, only two kinds of people drove them: burned-out hippies and VW enthusiasts. Oh, wait, that's just one kind of person. I was part of the other kind of people—broke graduate students.

When there weren't many Beetles on the road, why did I see them everywhere? Because I was **primed** to see them. Fiske and Taylor (1984) wrote,

"Recently and frequently accessed items come to mind more quickly than ideas that have not been activated." Here's what that means in plain English: because I was sitting in a VW Beetle, I was more prepared to see VW Beetles on the road.

You do the same thing in your car. Let's say you drive a Buick Encore. You are more likely to see Buick Encores than I am because you are primed to see them and I'm not. Because I never owned a Buick Encore and can't remember ever even sitting in one, I never notice them on the road. There is no priming for Buick Encores in my brain. Now, if Buick could invent a game that gets even non-Encore drivers looking for them and that raises their blood pressure doing it (e.g., Buick Bop or Encore Execution), then everyone would be primed for seeing Buick Encores. And when we look at the second mental error that results from priming, you'll see how this affects sales.

The second mental error I observed while driving my VW is called the **availability heuristic**. Two professors, Daniel Kahneman and Amos Tversky (1974, 1982), have outlined a number of mental shortcuts—called *judgmental heuristics*—used in making decisions in unclear situations. Dr. Tversky died in the 1990s. Dr. Kahneman won a Nobel Prize for the application of what you're learning here to economics. The availability heuristic is one type of judgmental heuristic that affects decisions, and it means that easy-to-remember events are seen as common or frequent.

For example, if I ask the average guy on the street, "Which is more common, words that start with the letter *k* or words that have *k* as the third letter?" most people decide that words that start with *k* are more common, even though the opposite is true. Why is this? Because it is easy to access (or think of) words that start with the letter *k* and hard to access (or think of) word that have the letter *k* as the third letter.

Slug Bug is another perfect example of this effect. Because pain is involved in the encoding of the event (priming), it is easy to recall; therefore, we assume that since it is easy to recall, VW Beetles must be very common (availability heuristic). Because I was (and still am) primed to see VW Beetles, I encoded them frequently (put them at the tippy top of my memory junk drawer). Therefore, those events were easier to remember, and I assumed they were very common. If I was asked how many VW Beetles there are in the United States, I would overestimate the number because it is easy for me to remember seeing them.

Finally, how does this apply to VW Beetle sales? When it comes time to buy a car, it is easier to remember VW Beetles and conclude that since everyone else is buying them—an effect called *social proof* (Cialdini, 2006)—they must be good. You want a good car, so you buy a VW Beetle. (Besides, it was all I could afford.)

The Evening News

Let's apply this to a more common thought pattern. Priming and the availability heuristic affect your daily thinking. Every night when you sit down to watch the evening news, you create a priming situation. You are encoding information about life that will affect how easily you remember it. The news dictum is "If it bleeds, it leads." In other words, if it is a graphic story with lots of good video footage—for example, a shooting, a fire, a car wreck, a flood, or other similar tragedy, then it will be the lead story. Such stories are far more entertaining than watching the mayor at a city council meeting announce a reduction in the crime rate. Violent or dramatic stories sink into your brain and train you to see violent and dramatic acts. When it comes time for you to estimate how dangerous the world is, you are more likely to remember the murder at the gas station in town than the announcement about the reduction in the crime rate. In fact, regular news watchers overestimate the frequency of violent crime, while those who don't watch the news have a more accurate estimation of crime rates (Romer, 2003).

If you think the world is a dark and evil place, it may be because you are filling your brain with easy-to-remember examples of the darkness and evil in the world. You are not filling your head with the more common (but far more mundane) examples of parents playing catch in the backyard with their kids. A mentor of mine, Roy Glass, was fond of saying, "Roger, some people like to chew on things that don't taste good."

The Publishers Clearing House Sweepstakes

Imagine I am walking down the street and I see a quarter on the sidewalk. As I bend down to pick it up, I see a TV image in the store window next to me. It's a clip of a Publishers Clearing House winner in her bathrobe screaming at the top of her lungs that she can't believe she won. She hugs the guy with the billboard-sized check, she cries, and then she thanks God and the fine folks at Publishers Clearing House (but not necessarily in that order). Then I look at the quarter on the sidewalk and think, *Just my luck, she gets $10 million, and I get a lousy quarter. My life stinks.*

If someone later asks me how lucky I am, I think, *I am not lucky. My life stinks.* I sink into a malaise. Why? Because I was primed to see the quarter as paltry, and I retrieved the available thought that when compared to others, I am not lucky.

Why is the windfall addition of 25 cents to my portfolio considered an unlucky thing? Because I got it in the context of someone else getting so much more. I was primed to see it as relatively paltry. Finding a quarter is a common occurrence and frankly not easy to remember. It makes you feel mildly positive but not ecstatically positive. Publishers Clearing House winners are easily available to remember even though they are extremely uncommon. Who doesn't remember a woman in a bathrobe jumping up and down on her doorstep after being told she is a millionaire? As a result, we overestimate the number of big-money winners.

Depressed people tend to see their lives as unhappy. When any event happens, they interpret this in the context of their unhappiness. Any event is then encoded as an example of their unhappiness. Heck, if they did win the $10 million, their first response would be, "Well, now I'm going to have to pay millions in taxes. That sucks!" When it comes time to think about the events of their lives, depressed people then find it easy to think about examples of how unhappy they are.

To change this mental priming and the availability heuristic is very difficult. First, people must change the kinds of information or entertainment they expose themselves to. If you are the kind of person who likes to watch TV shows and movies about tragedies, you are more likely to over-estimate the number of tragedies in the world and thus take a grimmer view of life. It is the same with watching the news. I gave up watching the news on a regular basis about the time the Hutus and Tutsis were hacking each other up with machetes in Rwanda. I was driving home from work in that VW Beetle listening to NPR reporting on the story. They were broadcasting audio of people butchering each other with machetes. I turned the radio off. I decided that inviting that tragedy in my life was too much. I could do more good helping the people nearby than I could for the people halfway around the world. I had had enough of chewing on things that don't taste good.

The second action people must take to change their mental priming and neutralize the availability heuristic is to think about beautiful, honorable, and praiseworthy things. To eliminate the depressing thoughts is not enough; they must be replaced by thinking about things that make you a better person. I don't pretend to be an authority on what is praiseworthy for everyone, but I'll tell you that if I see a beautiful painting or a picturesque mountainside, I feel better and happier.

Third, when people think back on their lives, they should always ask this checking question: Am I remembering all the events of my life or only the ones that are easy to remember? It is surely easier to remember dramatically bad events than to remember mundanely pleasant ones. Why is that? Because our brains are wired to protect us from danger (it tends to keep us alive).

If you have ever had food poisoning, you absolutely remember what it was that made you sick, and it is likely that you have never eaten it again. Why is that? Because your brain (and your tummy) is telling you to stay away from things that make you sick. But I'll bet that you can't remember what you had for dinner a week ago last Thursday. Why not? Because it was mildly positive. Our brains don't need to remember mildly positive. We do remember the ecstatically positive, but most of life is mildly positive—and unremarkable.

If you tend to find the cloud in every silver lining, you'll need to change the content of what you put in your head. If you want to help yourself become happy, search your memory and perhaps old photographs for glimpses of positive memories. You might be surprised at the happiness you'll find.

Mental Monkey

Every time you see a Volkswagen Beetle, remind yourself that your memory is subject to all sorts of errors. You can make yourself happier or more miserable depending on how you recall the events. (You can still play Slug Bug. It's okay. It's fun.)

Whenever you open the junk drawer in your kitchen, remind yourself that what you recently or frequently focus on will change how you remember your life.

Next time you tell the story of your food poisoning, try to recall what you had for dinner a week ago last Thursday. It was mildly positive and far more indicative of the food you usually eat than that egg salad at the church picnic.

What is the unpleasant association you make on a regular basis that makes you unhappy? _____
_____
_____What positive, praiseworthy thought could you use to replace it? _____
_____
_____ Whenever you see a VW Beetle or open your junk drawer, think that new, more positive thought!

Magic Act (Write This Down)

What **one** thing did I learn in this chapter that I can start applying now?

_____
_____
_____
_____

What **bad habit** of thinking do I want to change after reading this chapter?

_____

_____

_____

_____

_____

_____

_____

_____

What thing in my life will be my "**Mental Monkey**" (my reminder) that will help me to change my thinking from what I learned in this chapter?

_____

_____

_____

_____

_____

_____

_____

_____

What good place (like the Angel Waterfall) would I like to go to (in behavior or thought) but I haven't yet done the work to get there?

_____

_____

_____

_____

_____

_____

_____

_____

What reminders am I going to post to help me remember my new habit?

_____

_____

_____

_____

_____

_____

_____

_____

References

Cialdini, R.B. (2006). *Influence: The Psychology of Persuasion.* New York: William Morrow.

Fiske, S.T. & Taylor, S.E. (1984). *Social Cognition.* New York: Random House.

Kahneman, D. (2011). *Thinking, Fast and Slow.* Macmillan.

Kahneman, D., Slovic, S.P., Slovic, P. & Tversky, A. (Eds.). (1982). *Judgment Under Uncertainty: Heuristics and Biases.* Cambridge University Press.

Lewis, M. (2016). *The Undoing Project: A Friendship That Changed the World.* Penguin UK.

Romer, D., Jamieson, K.H. & Aday, S. (2003). Television news and the cultivation of fear of crime. *Journal of Communication, 53*(1), 88-104.

Tversky, A. & Kahneman, D. (1974). Judgment Under Uncertainty: Heuristics and Biases: Biases in Judgments Reveal Some Heuristics of Thinking Under Uncertainty. *Science, 185*(4157), 1124-1131.

⑨

WILDCAT IN THE WOODS

What a life-and-death chase with a wildcat can teach you about stress and health. You can protect your health if you're aware of the stress that can wear you down.

Do-It-Yourself Stress Tests

Have you ever heard someone say (or maybe even said yourself) something like, "You know, I read a thing that said being fired from your job is worth 50 points on a stress test."? To which you dutifully and earnestly replied, "Yeah, I read that somewhere, too." Chances are, you probably hadn't, but you, like bajillions of others, are sure you had heard it somewhere. And you are just as sure that a score of 50 is pretty bad. Well, such a test does in fact exist. It isn't just an urban legend. And being fired at work is really only worth 47 points.

But is a 47 really that bad? Who came up with this test? What does it mean? Okay, okay, I'll tell you. A 47 isn't actually that bad—if that is the only stressor in your life (which is unlikely). Researchers and psychiatrists Thomas Holmes and Richard Rahe came up with the stress test and called it the Holmes-Rahe Social Readjustment Rating Scale and published it in the *Journal of Psychosomatic Research* in 1967.

Over 50 years later, we're still using Holmes and Rahe's statistical model that correlates stressful life events with physical illness. In their model, a score of 300 or more raises the odds to about 80 percent that you will meet with what they call a major health breakdown. In other words, the more stressful your life, the more likely it is that you will get sick. In 1967, this was whizbang stuff. Holmes and Rahe were connecting a person's thinking with that person's physical illness.

We now know there is a strong connection between mental stress and physical illness.

In fact, some psychologists are making careers out of studying the relationship between emotional stress and physical health (e.g., Janice Kiecolt-Glaser at Ohio State University). And, most illnesses that the modern family physician treats could technically be called *mind-body diseases*. I'm not talking about Prozac treatments either.

Today, people in the Western world aren't dying of polio, beriberi, or smallpox (diseases from outside the body). They are dying of diabetes, high blood pressure, or heart attacks—mind-body diseases, all of which are related to stress. Now, don't get me wrong, I know there is a heritable component to these diseases, and 300 years ago we may not have seen high blood pressure frequently because people died first of smallpox. Having said that, our stressful lifestyles *are* killing us.

How exactly does this work? Well, this guy Hans Selye (a professor of biochemistry at McGill University in Toronto and one of the original researchers in the field of stress) came up with a model of how the body reacts to stress. In order to understand his model, it is important to know a little bit more about biology and neurobiology.

Okay, I confess. I know I promised I would get away from the neurobiology, but I can't help myself. And, after all, that last stuff wasn't so bad, was it? Plus, this is important.

In your body, you have two nervous systems working side by side all day long. They are called the *sympathetic* and *parasympathetic* nervous systems.

The **sympathetic nervous system** is the system that works when *emotions are charged*. You can remember this by remembering *sympathy* is an emotion and the sympathetic nervous system deals with amped-up emotions. So, when you are nervous or scared or sad or elated, the sympathetic nervous system is going to kick in. The sympathetic nervous system is the "fight, flight, faint, or freeze" nervous system.

What happens to your body when your sympathetic nervous system kicks in? Your pupils dilate, your heart rate goes up, adrenaline dumps into your bloodstream, your lungs dilate to increase their volume, and your body decreases skin blood flow (i.e., creates clammy palms). Another really cool thing is that the blood vessels in your arms and legs dilate. What this means is that the arteries that carry blood to your arms and legs expand, allowing them to carry more blood and the oxygen in it to move your arms and legs faster.

Imagine that you are using a garden hose to water your backyard garden. At the flip of a switch, the garden hose turns into a fire hose and the water pressure boosts to fire hydrant levels. You can imagine that the garden will get watered faster. The same thing happens in your arms and legs because of the sympathetic nervous system.

The **parasympathetic nervous system** is the *resting state nervous system*. When you are resting, the parasympathetic nervous system is kicking in. The parasympathetic is called the "rest, digest, and repair" nervous system. It is in charge of digestion, the constriction of the pupils, the slowing of the heartbeat, the slowing of breathing, and the increase of blood flow to the skin. During the activation of the parasympathetic nervous system, your body's resources are being directed to the immune system and to the production of T cells, which are good at healing injuries and illnesses. After Thanksgiving dinner, your parasympathetic nervous system is working overtime while you doze on the couch. You are warm, well fed, and relaxed, and even though you aren't even aware of it, your body is repairing itself (and the L-tryptophan in the turkey doesn't hurt either).

Here is the important point: The body has limited resources—when lots of activity is going on in one system, the other system shuts down. So when the sympathetic nervous system is activated to a high degree, there isn't enough energy to go around and as a result, the parasympathetic nervous system turns off. If you've ever had to give a speech and got nervous while waiting to walk up to the podium, you might have noticed that you got cottonmouth. It's that dry mouth that makes you think your tongue is stuck to the roof of your mouth. Why does that happen? I'm here to tell you. Your sympathetic nervous system turns on because you're anxious about the speech. Your parasympathetic nervous system turns off because there isn't enough fuel to go around. Saliva is the first part of digestion. When the parasympathetic nervous system turns off, so does digestion and saliva, hence cottonmouth. When you get cottonmouth, take a sip of water and be thankful that you got an extra jolt of adrenaline to kick it in your speech.

Wildcat in the Woods (Finally: The Story)

Let's say you are taking an autumn hike through the woods. You are looking at the leaves changing color on the trees when you see a wildcat off in the distance. You've seen them in pictures before but never in real life. Just like its photos on the internet, the wildcat has tan fur, dark tips on the ears, a long tail, and, you notice for the first time, it is nothing but muscle. At that same instant, the wildcat sees you. This never happened while watching those videos on your phone. Before you can blink, you realize that a blur of fur and teeth and claws is bolting toward you.

What do you do?

You have one of four options: (1) run away like crazy; (2) fight the wildcat; (3) faint; or (4) freeze. This is the classic fight, flight, faint, or freeze response. Unless you have sharp teeth and claws, I recommend running away. I've been told this is the wrong advice and that, in fact, wildlife experts say fighting is better. (More on the fight/anger response in the next chapter.)

Whichever response you choose, your body must prepare for it. Fortunately, you don't have to think about preparing for it. Deep structures in your limbic system (remember that middle part of your brain that coordinates the activities of the brain and regulates emotions?) are already getting it done. Within the blink of an eye, your sympathetic nervous system is working overtime.

You know the physical jolt you feel when you are startled by a loud noise? Well, that is your first-round blast from your sympathetic nervous system. In the fight-or-flight response, your body is preparing to either fight or run away. In order to do either of these things, you need the muscles in your arms and legs to function at maximum capacity. Your muscles use three things as fuel: sugar, oxygen, and adrenaline. The purpose of the sympathetic nervous system is to get those three things to your muscles as quickly as possible in as large a quantity as possible.

The moment you recognize that the furball of death is hurtling at you, the pupils of your eyes dilate (expand). This allows you to use all the available light to see as clearly as possible. You need to see the wildcat to know what you are running away from. As you turn to run, your arteries have already dilated—they've turned from puny garden hoses to fire hoses to take blood packed with sugar, oxygen, and adrenaline (i.e., the fuel) to the muscles of the arms and legs to help you to run.

The bronchioles and alveolae (the big and little tubes) of the lungs have dilated so that the surface area of your lungs has increased. The surface area of your lungs is about the size of a tennis court (I learned that from Bill Nye the Science Guy). All that surface area allows lots of oxygen to travel to your bloodstream and then to your muscles. The adrenaline being dumped from your adrenal glands is already coursing through your arteries. Adrenaline is your body's version of amphetamine. It gives you an immediate boost of energy and power.

That immediate burst of speed allows you to run faster than you have ever run before. The wildcat, seeing you as a delicious, tender dinner, increases acceleration. As the wildcat gains on you, you notice a river ahead. Ignoring the cold, you dive into the icy river and swim across while the wildcat stops on the shore, hesitant because of the water. (I don't know if it is true for wildcats, but for the purposes of our story, wildcats hate swimming.) As you drag yourself to the other side, you turn, shivering from the cold, and look at the wildcat pacing on the opposite shore. You shake your fist in the air and yell something silly like, "I showed you, you stupid wildcat, you couldn't get me! Ha!" At that point, you break into a jog to keep yourself warm and head for home. While you are at home, wrapped in a blanket, sipping hot chocolate and with your feet in a pan of warm water, you regale your family with the tale of your adventure. You're still excited by your narrow escape, and you tell and retell your story to as many as will listen.

All of this makes for a pretty decent story—the kind you'll tell your grand-children. But what in the heck does this have to do with stress tests?

Let's look at what happened in your body as you made your escape from the furball of death. Your sympathetic nervous system went into overdrive to help you escape. At the same time, the parasympathetic nervous system turned off. When you were running away from the wildcat, you didn't need to be digesting that cheeseburger that was your lunch, because if you didn't move, you would *be* lunch. Your body didn't need to fight that mild bacterial infection in your sinuses because a mild bacterial infection isn't as great a threat to your life as wildcat claws and teeth. The resources you needed for maintaining your body (parasympathetic) were diverted to saving your body (sympathetic).

Something else happened in your brain. Before seeing the wildcat, you were mentally composing a poem for your beloved. While you were hur-dling bushes like an Olympian, you didn't need to do abstract thinking for the future (like creating love poems). All your brain's resources were directed to staying alive right now!

During the run and swim, almost all the oxygen, sugar, and adrenaline that dumped into your arteries were used up by your muscles. The little bit of adrenaline and blood sugar left in your system was used up when you yelled and shook your fist at the wildcat and jogged home. As you approached your house, your jog turned into a walk. By the time you were at your front door, your breathing returned pretty much to normal. Your sympathetic nervous system, having done its job, takes a rest. At this

WILDCAT IN THE WOODS

point, the parasympathetic nervous system gears back up to rest, digest, and repair the body. You promptly take a nap.

The system works like a charm when you are doing things like running away from wildcats or killing woolly mammoths. But if you think about it, not many people have to run away from wild animals or chase behemoths with spears for dinner anymore. The stressors we deal with are of a completely different kind. Most of the stress we experience comes not from outside threats but from the inside—our thinking. Furthermore, the mental stressors we experience are not over quickly; they tend to be long-lasting stressors.

Wildcat Versus the Boss's Opinion

The stressors most people experience today are more like this: You walk into the office the morning after you completed a big report for your boss. This proposal is your shining moment. After you arrived home last night, you told your spouse that when your boss sees this proposal, you are going to land a big raise.

So there you sit in your office, waiting for your boss to come in. You fantasize about your boss bursting through the door with the proposal in hand, sweating from excitement, saying, "Jones, this is the best idea this company has had in 40 years! You need a raise and a big promotion. Let's go to lunch and talk about your bright future in the company."

You fidget at your desk, anticipating the glorious moment. And you wait. Then 9:30 rolls around—no boss. You call his assistant. "Yes, he is in the office." So you wait and fidget. You ask yourself, "Is he reading it? What if he doesn't like it?" You reread your copy. "Did I say something stupid?" You find a typo on the eighth page and internally kick yourself. "You are so stupid. How could you turn in a proposal with such an obvious mistake?" You check your email. Nothing. You check your voicemail. Nothing. You try to work on something else, but you are distracted. Soon, 11:45 ticks by. Still no smiling boss coming through the door. Your stomach begins to gurgle. You reach for the Tums. You pace around your office. You check your email again. You begin to debate the merits of a late lunch because your boss might come by after you leave. You resolve that you will go to lunch at 1:00. You wait. Nothing.

You call his assistant again. "Yes, he is in the office. No, it isn't clear whether he has read your proposal." At 12:59 you walk out the door. Down the hall, you see your boss. He's heading your way. This is it; this is your moment. When he is four feet away, he looks up and smiles—your heart races, and then you realize he isn't looking at you, he's smiling at the person behind you. He didn't even acknowledge you. In your head you think, *Oh my gosh. He's ignoring me. He deliberately snubbed me. Oh, my goodness. He thinks my proposal stank. My days here are numbered. I have to begin looking for another job. What was I thinking? Why did I ever pin my hopes on that idea?*

As you chew your cheeseburger and take a swig of Maalox, you mull over your future. In your mind, you are writing out your letter of resignation. You are thinking, *How am I going to pay the mortgage?* You write down a list of companies that might be hiring. As you ride the elevator back to your floor, your mind is a swirl of confusion and fear. You spend the rest of the afternoon writing out your letter of resignation and place it in the drawer. You rehearse all the things you would like to tell your boss once you quit. At 4:45, you stop by his assistant's desk and ask if the boss has had a chance to read your proposal. His assistant sorts through a stack and there, in the middle, is your unread proposal. "No, he hasn't looked at any of this stuff yet. He might get to it next week." You mumble thanks and turn to shuffle out.

Each day of the next week is alternately spent brooding about your dire circumstances or your bright future. You buy an extra bottle of Maalox. You aren't sleeping well, so you wash down a sleeping pill with a shot of bourbon. Compared to all that, running from a wildcat might seem preferable . . .

The General Adaptation Syndrome and You

Wildcats are much less common than the prolonged mental stressors that we face today. Unfortunately, our bodies are geared for wildcats, not for bosses who don't read our proposals. Hans Selye, the father of the study of stress, came up with the notion that if you have prolonged stress, the body goes through three identifiable stages, a process which he called the **general adaptation syndrome (GAS)**. It is an imperfect theory (there are plenty of neuroscientists who will quibble with a model that is over 60 years old), but it is an elegant analogy for our purposes.

The *alarm stage* of the general adaptation syndrome is what happens when you see the wildcat or when you first walk into the office the morning after submitting a big proposal. The surprise and anxiety caused by the new situation result in the activation of the sympathetic nervous system. Blood flows to the extremities. There is a commensurate decrease in injury healing and digestion. The increased blood flow to the arms and legs results in a decreased blood flow to the stomach and intestines. There is an increased heart rate and dilated lung capacity. No problem.

The *resistance stage* occurs when the body is fighting the stressor for a prolonged period of time but is unable to maintain that level of activation. Because the immune system is impaired, the body is more susceptible to disease. Bodily maintenance functions are lower and slower because there are no extra resources available to do the work.

With a wildcat, you never get to the resistance stage. You either escape or get eaten. In the world where most of us live, your stomach begins to rumble when you eat. You get heartburn. You are wired at bedtime because of the extra blood sugar and adrenaline in your system. Your body is pumping cortisol (a stress hormone that reduces inflammation in the short run) into your bloodstream as a reaction to stress. Plaques begin to build up on the walls of your coronary arteries. In the resistance stage, your body is essentially running on adrenaline. It is not a sustainable state. Your body is teetering on the edge of collapse.

In the *exhaustion stage*, your body finally gives out. The bodily systems that are used for the resting state have had no resources to do their job, so your body eventually succumbs to opportunistic diseases, like ulcers, diabetes, heart disease, and cancer (remember all those mind-body diseases we talked about earlier?). You have an extra load of cortisol in your system.

We know that its presence in the blood is related to post-traumatic stress disorder, anxiety, and depression.

In prolonged stressful situations, your body will give out and you will experience a serious health crisis simply because your body is not made for prolonged stressors. I remember in college, one of the big complaints people had after Christmas or spring break was that they were sick the whole time. We'd talk about what a bummer it was to be sick during vacation, but in retrospect, I see what was happening. Students would tear their bodies up by staying up too late, not resting, worrying about grades, and studying (okay, some of them were partying). By the end of the term, their bodies were in the tail-end of the resistance stage. Fueled mostly by adrenaline and caffeine, many students would take their last final exam. Once the stressor was over, the body could collapse in exhaustion, and they would become sick over vacation.

This may have happened to you even after college. I've met dozens of people who complain that they must have caught something on the airplane on the way to their beach vacation. That may very well be true (probably not), but more likely overwork set them up for a collapse on vacation.

So many of our stressors are mental. But as we think about a stressful situation, our body reacts as if it were the real situation. Our imagination of the stressful event can evoke in our brains the same cascade of chemicals that seeing a wildcat in the woods can. You can think of the many times you have worried about things over a long period of time—each time, that worry initiates the brain (and your body) to prepare for the wildcat. In fact, you may be worrying right now if you'll respond to a wildcat attack in the best way. That worry may create worse problems than a real wildcat chasing you (provided you get away).

So, What Do I Do?

Worry is different from fear. Worry is future tense. Worry is *anticipatory* fear. With worry, your body does no fighting or fleeing. Your body fills up with all the chemistry that it would when you are needing to run from the wildcat, but you are just sitting at your desk. Fear is present tense and you have the same four options for your response: fight (or anger), flight (run away), faint, or freeze. Each of these is, in its own way, adaptive to a threat.

If you are afraid or worrying while you are sitting at your desk, you can activate your parasympathetic nervous system by doing deep diaphragmatic breathing. You can hijack the sympathetic response by consciously breathing as you would in the parasympathetic phase. You do this by breathing from your stomach. Don't try to expand your chest, expand your belly when you breathe. This moves the diaphragm and can activate the parasympathetic response. To learn how, look into the resources at the end of this chapter.

Fear and anger are very similar physiological responses to the same threat appraisal. Both dump nearly identical chemicals into our systems as a response to the wildcat. What if your primary response isn't flight (fear), but is anger (fight)?

Unfortunately, we rarely do the things we need to do to eliminate all that mentally generated chemistry.

But that leads right into the next chapter: The History of Kitchen Appliances.

Mental Monkey

 Next time you are browsing through *National Geographic* magazine or looking at YouTube videos or on Instagram and see a photo of a wildcat or cougar, remind yourself of how your body reacts to stress. Remind yourself that prolonged stress can make you sick.

When you watch the news, pay attention to how you feel. Then count the number of medicines that are advertised. Have you ever noticed that news program advertisers are usually drug companies selling medicines to treat mind-body diseases such as blood pressure, depression, irritable bowel syndrome, heartburn, and more?

When you see an advertisement for blood pressure medicine or look at a bottle of antacid, remind yourself that these are mind-body diseases that can be controlled by changing the way we deal with the wildcat in the woods.

Next time you are brooding about the upcoming meeting with your boss, remember the stew of chemicals you are pouring into your body.

When that cheeseburger doesn't sit well in your stomach, monitor your thoughts as you reach for the Tums.

The Magic Act (Write This Down)

What **one** thing did I learn in this chapter that I can start applying now?

_____

_____

_____

What **bad habit** of thinking do I want to change after reading this chapter?

_____

_____

_____

_____

_____

_____

_____

_____

What thing in my life will be my "**Mental Monkey**" (my reminder) that will help me to change my thinking from what I learned in this chapter?

_____

_____

_____

_____

_____

_____

_____

_____

What good place (like the Angel Waterfall) would I like to go to (in behavior or thought) but I haven't yet done the work to get there?

_____

_____

_____

_____

_____

_____

_____

What reminders am I going to post to help me remember my new habit?

_____

_____

_____

_____

_____

_____

_____

_____

References

Brown, R. & Gerbarg, P. (2012). *The Healing Power of the Breath: Simple Techniques to Reduce Stress and Anxiety, Enhance Concentration, and Balance Your Emotions*. Shambhala Publications.

Chen, Y.F., Huang, X.Y., Chien, C.H. & Cheng, J.F. (2017). The effectiveness of diaphragmatic breathing relaxation training for reducing anxiety. *Perspectives in Psychiatric Care, 53*(4), 329-336.

Glaser, R. & Kiecolt-Glaser, J.K. (2005). Stress-induced immune dysfunction: implications for health. *Nature Reviews Immunology, 5*(3), 243-251.

Greenberger, D. & Padesky, C.A. (2015). *Mind Over Mood, Second Edition: Change How You Feel by Changing the Way You Think*. The Guilford Press.

Holmes, T.H. & Rahe, R.H. (1967). The social readjustment rating scale. *Journal of Psychosomatic Research, 11*(2), 213-218.

Jerath, R., Crawford, M.W., Barnes, V.A. & Harden, K. (2015). Self-regulation of breathing as a primary treatment for anxiety. *Applied Psychophysiology and Biofeedback, 40*(2), 107-115.

Kiecolt-Glaser, J.K. & Newton, T.L. (2001). Marriage and health: his and hers. *Psychological Bulletin, 127*(4), 472.

LeDoux, J.E. (2015). *Anxious: Using the Brain to Understand and Treat Fear and Anxiety*. Penguin.

Levi, M., Bossù, M., Luzzi, V., Semprini, F., Salaris, A., Ottaviani, C., Violani, C. & Polimeni, A. (2022). Breathing out dental fear: A feasibility crossover study on the effectiveness of diaphragmatic breathing in children sitting on the dentist's chair. *International Journal of Paediatric Dentistry,* February 13. https://doi.org/10.1111/ipd.12958

Ma, X., Yue, Z.Q., Gong, Z.Q., Zhang, H., Duan, N.Y., Shi, Y.T., Wei, G.X. & Li, Y.F. (2017). The effect of diaphragmatic breathing on attention, negative affect and stress in healthy adults. *Frontiers in Psychology, 8*, 874.

Selye, H. (1978). *The Stress of Life,* Second Edition. McGraw Hill.

Selye, H. (2013). *Stress in Health and Disease*. Butterworth-Heinemann.

Uchino, B.N., Cacioppo, J.T. & Kiecolt-Glaser, J.K. (1996). The relationship between social support and physiological processes: a review with emphasis on underlying mechanisms and implications for health. *Psychological Bulletin, 119*(3), 488.

THE HISTORY OF KITCHEN APPLIANCES

What the vagaries of pressure cookers teach us about handling stress and what happens when you don't control your anger. It can help you understand the difference between the **form and the content of anger**, and how to productively control the negative tendencies anger can create.

Homework at the Kitchen Table

My life is full of mundane memories, most of which would bore you, and perhaps this one will too—however, it makes a nice introduction to this chapter. I remember many days sitting at the kitchen table, leaning over my homework while my mother cooked dinner. On a winter evening in the late 1970s, I remember doing algebra or trigonometry while my mom made pot roast. Looking out the window, it was already dark, and she was about to have me clear my books and start setting the table.

I was not particularly looking forward to dinner because (and this might have been a surprise to my mom) I hated pot roast. You see, my mom used to make pot roast in a pressure cooker. (I should add that my mother is a great cook, but my family has a way of only remembering the one or two dishes that were duds.) If you've never had a meal cooked in an old-school pressure cooker, then you are lucky (great, now I've made all the pressure cooker manufacturers mad at me). I'm not talking about the high-tech cookers of the Instant Pot variety, but the ones with steel lids that you had to twist to lock into place and that were topped with a pressure-release valve that made a slight hissing noise for the duration of the cooking time. The potatoes and carrots that come out of such a contraption are slightly more gelatinous than mush. The pot roast . . . uh, how can I best describe it? I used to pull off the strings of meat and line them up in rows on my plate. But enough on a bad meal.

The thing I remember is the "chika chika chika chika chika chika" sound of the pressure cooker. If you don't know how pressure cookers work, read on. Essentially, you put food and water in a sealed pot and heat it, and the steam that builds up raises the pressure inside the pot. The increased pressure allows for boiling at a lower temperature and more thorough cooking in a shorter period of time. Makers of pressure cookers promise that you can take a nickel cut of beef and turn it into prime rib in half an hour (see meal description above for a rebuttal). The "chika chika" sound came from steam escaping from under a weighted valve on the lid of the pot. As I looked across the kitchen to the stove, I remember seeing little puffs of steam escaping from the lid that wafted the smell of chewy pot roast through the house. When the food was finished cooking, my mom would take a wooden spoon and tap a button on the lid of the pot, and thereby shoot an enormous cloud of steam across the stove and into the middle of the kitchen.

Little did I know that 300 years earlier, Denis Papin of England had invented the pressure cooker, which he called a *steam digester*. (I think the name change from steam digester to pressure cooker was a wise marketing move.) The little weighted "chika chika" valve and the steam button on the top were designed to make sure that the pressure cooker never built up enough pressure to explode.

According to Charles Panati in his book, *The Extraordinary Origins of Everyday Things*, (1987):

> History's first pressure cooker bombed—figuratively and literally. Not only did the majority of Londoners not take favorably to the idea of steamed pike and pigeon, but those who purchased a digester and

attempted its recipes often ended up with the evening's meal on the kitchen wall. The temperature vicissitudes of an open fire were no match for Papin's imperfect safety valve. Several serious accidents were reported. (p. 122)

I love that—"several serious accidents were reported." I'll bet the sales guys decided to make a career change when that hit the newspapers.

It is no wonder that when people talk about a tough workplace or a bad situation, they talk about it being a pressure cooker. If you work or live in a pressure cooker long enough, you are going to explode. It seems to me that there are two ways of keeping the pressure cooker from exploding:

1. Let off steam
2. Turn off the fire

The same goes for controlling anger.

Anger and Letting Off Steam

There is a pretty substantial controversy about the effectiveness of letting off steam. Some researchers will say that venting, or catharsis, only leads to more anger and or violence. In some sense, they're right. They'd argue that a nice leisurely walk in the country rather than a hard run will calm you down and vent off the anger. I would agree that they may be right, but only when venting is done incorrectly (and it usually is done incorrectly).

When I was a kid and got angry, my mom or dad would have me mow the lawn. When I was mad, the only thing I liked about mowing the lawn to exorcise my anger was pulling the starter cord on the mower. Sometimes I'd hope the stupid thing wouldn't start. If I was angry, it was very satisfying to yank on that cord, mutter unspeakables, and yank it again. While I was mowing neat little rows in the backyard, all I could do was imagine spinning, hands gripped around the handle of the mower, and hurling it like the Olympic hammer throw across the yard and into the bushes. Yeah, that seemed like it would get my anger out. Destroying something, I thought, would make me less angry. After an hour of such fantasy, I'd be pretty worn out from mowing and was finally able to think clearly.

In the hour of mowing, I used up all the extra chemistry that I had created in my body by being angry (remember the Wildcat in the Woods chapter?). Mowing the lawn was a really great way to vent my anger. At the end, the yard is mowed (a productive activity) and I am worn out (burning out my anger). Hurling the mower, though it seemed enticing, would have been the incorrect way to vent anger.

The reason that much of catharsis, or venting, doesn't work is because it is not done correctly. If someone gets mad, they often go around and break stuff. It seems that for men, cordless electronic devices are the most popular. I couldn't tell you how many men have told me about the remote controls they've broken in anger. I think the universal remote-control market exists primarily because men throw and stomp so many remotes in anger. Men have similar reactions with cell phones. The devices have the same heft as a small rock but make an apparently much more satisfying sound as they smash against the wall. Nonetheless, tossing your iPhone is a bad idea if you want to productively deal with anger.

Letting Off Steam Just Messes Up the Kitchen

There is a goodly amount of research (and common sense) that will tell you that breaking things to let off steam will actually increase your level of anger. I would contend the same goes for verbal catharsis. First, let's talk about yelling. Yelling initially feels good because you are directing all your adrenaline-induced anger through your voice, and you rationalize (tell yourself rational lies) that no one is getting hurt. Waving your fists, slamming doors, and hollering is immediately emotionally satisfying, but in the end, you are usually just as angry as you were before. The people who got to witness the anger are now creating their own internal chemistry and becoming angry or agitated as well (just the recipe for a good fight).

Now let's consider talking about your anger rather than yelling. Sitting around talking angrily with someone about why you are angry will initially increase your anger (because you are mentally reliving it) and then temporarily decrease your anger (because you have talked about it). Ultimately, however, the anger returns (because you have practiced being angry for a long period of time by talking about it and not doing anything about it). I don't want to take away from talking to a friend or trusted confidante about your anger, but it is an incomplete solution.

There are two parts to successfully controlling anger:

1. reducing the physical chemistry
2. increasing mental discipline

PC-PEPA: Chopping Firewood Eliminates the Physical Chemistry

To address the physical chemistry, I propose what I call *perfectly controlled productive, explosive physical activity*—one client called it *PC-PEPA*. Think *politically correct pepper*. That'll help you remember. You know the kind of pepper I'm talking about—the kind that was coaxed to give up its pepper life at the hands of gentle Birkenstock-wearing hippies only to be used as a garnish on endive salad among peace-loving people everywhere. (Please, no letters from Birkenstock-wearing hippies in the pepper business. I'm actually doing you a favor. Remember, by connecting your work to anger management in this book, I'm probably increasing the sales of your product by priming the readers to think about ethically produced pepper. You can thank me later.)

Perfectly controlled productive, explosive physical activity (PC-PEPA) is not about breaking things; it's about doing something constructive that physically uses up all the chemistry your body has produced in your anger. The perfect example of a PC-PEPA is chopping wood. If you become angry, chopping wood is a great way to use up all that extra chemistry.

Here's why: First, chopping wood uses up a lot of energy. If you have excess blood sugar and adrenaline coursing through your veins, chopping half a cord of logs will certainly use it all up.

Second, chopping wood is **explosive**. Swinging that ax full force on a piece of timber focuses that anger. The loud crack of the wood splitting satisfies the desire for loud sound. It isn't like mowing the lawn, where the repetitive tracing of the yard eventually wears you out; it is an explosive physical activity.

Third, it is **productive**. Unlike breaking the remote or putting your fist through the drywall, at the end of your angry period, you have produced something useful. You've got firewood you can use and enjoy in the fireplace.

Fourth, and probably most importantly, throughout the whole exercise you must exert physical and mental discipline. You must perfectly control every swing. If you get mad and start swinging the ax around wildly, you will end up cutting off your toe. As a result, your anger must be reined in, directed, and consciously and **perfectly controlled**. The end result is that you learn to control your anger. And that is the goal.

You may be thinking to yourself, *I don't have a fireplace. What am I supposed to do?* There are lots of other things you can do. I've talked to dozens of people who don't want to chop wood but want to control their anger. Here are some other ideas:

- *Scrubbing the bathtub.* This is not my favorite, but I understand that the pressure applied to the tub with the grit of the cleanser really helps some people.

- *Running.* The pounding of each footfall on the pavement is like a tiny explosion, and the satisfaction of the miles slipping past under your feet can feel productive.

- *Hitting a boxing bag.* If you want to build upper body strength while combating anger, hitting a 40-pound punching bag should do the trick. Let me add one point—buy gloves or at least tape your hands before starting. I assigned this activity to a young man, and he came back into my office the next week with huge scabs on his hands. I asked what happened, and he said the friction of the bag on his hands cut him up pretty badly. I asked him why he hadn't stopped. He said because it was too satisfying.

- *Hitting golf balls on the driving range.* If you are a golfer, this is a great option.

- *Hitting baseballs at the batting cage.*

- *Practicing hockey slap shots against the side of the local elementary school.*
- *Smacking racquetballs, handballs, or tennis balls against the garage door.*

Now we get to the perfectly controlled part. If you are hitting golf balls, you can't just hit for distance. You have to swing for accuracy. Otherwise, you are training your body and your brain to **not** control your anger. If you do not have perfect control of your anger, you are just having a temper tantrum.

Turning Off the Fire: The Mental Discipline of Anger

Before you go out and break your favorite driver on the driving range or bloody your hands on a boxing bag, let's talk about the mental discipline involved in PC-PEPA. If you don't integrate the mental control of PC-PEPA, all you have is wild-eyed crazy anger—a kind of anger that you've rationalized because you read it was okay in someone else's book.

There are some mental caveats to PC-PEPA you should keep in mind.

1. **No negative mental rehearsal is allowed.** If you imagine hitting, punching, or chopping the mental image of a person while you do the PC-PEPA, you lose all of the benefit. You don't want to imagine the person you are angry at with his or her head on the log you are splitting or their face on the punching bag.

    I worked with a person who had a computer program that made computer-generated bullet holes (with the attendant gunshot noise) on his screen with each mouse click. When angry with his wife, he would simply make her photo be the background on his computer screen and shoot imaginary bullet holes in her face. This is precisely the opposite of what I am suggesting.

2. **When angry, do not create unnecessary fear in innocent bystanders.** Your children can see you chopping wood or hitting baseballs, but if your physical activity is not perfectly controlled and you create fear in your kids, you lose the benefit of PC-PEPA.

When innocent bystanders become afraid, then your anger is not perfectly controlled.

At this point, some of you are saying: "Man, with all these rules about anger, it is too hard to do. When I am angry, I can't control myself."

You know how I answer that? "You're lying to yourself."

The biggest lie we tell ourselves about anger is this: "I lost my temper." What? Did you leave it in your other pants? Is it out in the car? You never lose your temper. You *decide* to become angry. Let me prove it to you.

The Telephone Test

Have you ever been in an argument with a loved one at home with hollering and name calling—or at least raised voices? Here's how it goes:

Angry Person 1: You lousy, no-good bum. I wish I never married your sorry carcass. My mother was right. You are a loser!

Angry Person 2: Oh yeah, well you ought to talk! Talk about losers. You are the queen of losers!

(Phone rings. Angry Person 2 picks up.)

Angry Person 2 *(sweetly)*: Hello . . . oh hi, how are you? Yeah, yeah, oh, I'm sorry, she can't come to the phone right now *(silently mouthing the words "Shut up. SHUT UP! I hate you!")*. Can I have her call you back? Sure. How are the kids? Great. Hey, I'm glad you called. I'll be sure to give her the message. Uh-huh. Bye now.

(Hang up.)

Angry Person 2: Shut up. Shut UP! Can't you see I was on the phone? You are so rude! Get out of my face and get out of my life.

Now if you are smiling even a little bit at this, you have failed what I call the *telephone test*. We *all* have failed the telephone test. What the telephone test proves is that we are all in control of our anger. We can, at the sound of a little ringtone, change our vocal tone, the content of what we are saying, and our whole demeanor—because we decide to.

When you become angry at a loved one,
you are deciding to become angry.

You are deciding how and when you are becoming angry. For those of you who still say you can't control your temper, I tell you that you can—however, you are lousy at it. With practice, you can succeed.

Let me give you another example: For some reason, some men like to punch walls when they are angry. I went to high school with a guy who liked to put his head through a wall when he was angry. Someone told me his garage walls were full of head-butt holes. In all the time I have been working with men who like to punch walls, I have very rarely known a guy to break his hand while doing so. Why is this? When a wall puncher is about to do the deed, in the milliseconds between the time he decides to hit the wall and he actually hits the wall, he is making a number of decisions. First, he is judging the composition of the wall. Wall punchers know they will break their hands on concrete block. So he is choosing which wall is made of drywall.

Second, in those milliseconds he is also doing a mathematical estimation. A drywall puncher knows that if he hits a part of the wall with a stud directly behind it, he will break his hand. If we say that the studs are two inches wide and set 16 inches on center, and the width of his hand is four inches, then there is about a one in four chance that a man hitting the wall will hit a stud and thus break his hand. My experience suggests that the number of wall punchers who break their hand is far less than one in four.

As a result, I have concluded that wall punchers, from the time they are drawing back their fists to the time they land the punch, are sizing up where the studs are. They are thinking; they are planning the punches. They are deciding to punch the wall. They are in control of the punch and thus in control of how they express their anger. When they say they can't control themselves, they are lying to themselves to rationalize their wrong behavior.

Let me give another example. People in their anger usually don't break irreplaceable things (thus the high percentage of broken remote controls). And if they do break some one-of-a-kind thing, there is usually a reason. A woman who breaks a family heirloom that her husband has on the fireplace mantle breaks it not because she couldn't control herself but because she wanted to break precisely that thing to punish her husband.

When I was 3 or 4, I threw a temper tantrum and broke a clay pinch pot that my sister had received as a gift. It was irreplaceable. I hadn't intended to break the pinch pot, but at 3 or 4, I decided to become angry. I decided to start stomping and whirling around. I wasn't after the ill-fated pinch pot, but I did decide to make my arms and legs swing wildly. My decisions broke that pinch pot. I had decided to become physically angry, and the natural consequence of a preschooler tantrum is something breaking.

When we become angry, it is because we decide to become angry or have practiced becoming angry for so long that it is almost automatic. Either way, if you decide to become angry in an instant or have decided hundreds of times to become angry in the past, you made the decision to become angry.

Form Versus Content of Anger

I think now is a good time to differentiate the form of anger from the content of anger. You may have the idea that I am anti-anger. I am not. I am arguing for anger that is both for the right reason and expressed in the right way.

The **content** of your anger is the reason you become angry. Imagine, for example, that I have told my 3-year-old daughter not to run in the street because she could get hit by a car and killed. One afternoon, she runs in the street and is nearly hit by a car. In my initial fear, let's say I become angry (the transfer of one negative emotion to another is pretty common). That is the *content* of my anger. Lots of people would say my anger is understandable. Lots of reasonable people would become angry at the same situation.

Now use the same example to understand the **form** of my anger (the way I express my anger). Imagine I scold her in a harsh tone. Lots of people would say that my anger is understandable. Lots of reasonable people scold their children for running in the street. Let's say (and I would never really do this—I am only using it for an example) I drag her by her hair from the street into the front yard and beat her with a stick. Lots of reasonable people would say I was a monster. Why? They are not criticizing the content of my anger, but they are critical of the form of my anger. (In case you are worried about my daughter, this is just an illustration. Nothing like this has ever happened in real life. She is a grown up now, so don't call the county.)

All too often when we are angry, we refuse to ask for forgiveness for our anger or admit our wrongdoing. We think that if we admit that the *form* of our anger was wrong, we are admitting that the *content* of our anger was wrong. I think when you become angry, you will want to ask for forgiveness if either the form or content of your anger was wrong. But if the content of your anger was correct (and I think there are cases when you ought to be angry), you should be willing to recant the form of your anger when it is wrong (destructive, disproportionate to the problem, at the incorrect person).

At the end of all this, you may be thinking that controlling anger is still hard *and* that all these rules make it harder. No kidding. You're in good company. Here's what Aristotle said:

> "Anyone can become angry—that is easy, but to be angry with the right person to the right degree, at the right time, for the right purpose, and in the right way—this is not easy." (*Nicomachean Ethics*)

If you have trouble with anger (either in form or content), you are in good company. Keep struggling. It is only through the struggle to control both the form and the content of your anger that you gain mastery over it.

The Anger Volcano

Think about the angry explosion as the top of a volcano. As you look at the volcano, consider one side of the hill leading up to the explosion and the other side of the hill leading away (down) from the explosion. Most anger management courses focus on the buildup to anger—we'll call this the left side of the anger volcano. In fact, this was part of my training, and I taught the same things in the early years of my practice. Here's how the textbook conversation goes between the therapist and the angry client:

Therapist: So tell me, what led up to you being angry?

Angry Client: Well, I woke up this morning and as I was getting out of bed, I stubbed my toe. Then as I was walking to the bathroom, I stepped on the cat's tail and the cat scratched me. Then my kids all took showers before me and I ran out of hot water in the shower. Then I spilled coffee on my new tie. That made me late for work, so I got caught in traffic. So by the time I arrived to work, I was already frazzled. Then I knew I had a presentation with my boss, but the printer was on the fritz so I couldn't print out my talking points. Then my coworker Bob started joking around with me. I just lost it (see, here is the subtle lie again).

Therapist: (soothingly) Good, good. Now let's retrace the steps you took this morning. Okay, when you stubbed your toe, you needed to take a cleansing breath and count to 10. When you step on the cat's tail, you have to tell yourself, "It's only an innocent animal that didn't know any better." When you run out of hot water, you need to remind yourself of the blessing of having children. (And so on.)

In my experience, the conversation actually goes like this:

Therapist: So tell me, what led up to you being angry?

Angry Client: I don't know, I felt fine and then I just popped.

Therapist: Did you step on a cat's tail? Did your kids use up all the hot water? Did you spill coffee on your tie?

Angry Client: Uh . . . no, no, and uh, no.

Therapist: Give me a minute. I have to look this one up in the book.

What I found is that most angry people haven't got a clue as to what led up to their anger. Furthermore, in most cases, the goal of anger management is to keep people from being angry. That is not my goal. My goal is Aristotle's goal—anger in the right amount, to the right degree, at the right time, at the right person, and for the right purpose. There are times when you should be angry, but perfectly controlled, disciplined anger is rare. I've been angry six times in the last 24 hours. I've been angry the way Aristotle describes approximately six times in my entire life.

What is more helpful is looking at the right side of the anger volcano—the cooling-down side. There are two important points as people cool from their explosion: the first is the point at which their conscience kicks in and tells them (with Jiminy Cricket's voice), "You were out of line." For some people, it occurs in the midst of the explosion; for others, it is a few seconds or minutes later. For even others, it may be hours, days, weeks, months, or years before their conscience tells them they were out of line. The second point comes later. This is the point at which they ask for forgiveness for the form and/or the content of their anger. Again, just like the conscience, this could take minutes, hours, days, weeks, months, or years. My least favorite response is "Never."

Take note of the words I've chosen here. I didn't say the point at which they said they were sorry, I said the point at which they *ask forgiveness*. Why do I make this distinction? For two very important reasons: First, if you have kids, you know that even in the midst of anger, an angry child can say he or she is sorry.

Mom: "Tell your brother you are sorry."

Child: (Growling) "I'm sorry." (The words were accompanied by a stuck-out tongue.)

Second, the words "I'm sorry" are not the admission of personal responsibility in our society. Let me give you an example.

Imagine you and I are in a crowded elevator. You're standing right behind me. At the second floor, the doors open, a bunch of people get off, and more people get on the elevator. I step backward and onto your toe. What do I say? Ninety-five percent of the people I've asked have said the following:

Me: "I'm sorry."

You: "That's okay."

Have I admitted that I willfully and intentionally stepped on your toe? No. What the combination of "I'm sorry" and "That's okay" means in our society is this:

Me: "I'm sorry." (Isn't it too bad what just now happened?)

You: "That's okay." (Yes, it is.)

That is all "I'm sorry" and "that's okay" means in our society.

Let's imagine we change the situation a little. The next day, you and I are both in the elevator alone. I had so much fun yesterday stepping on your toe that today I do it on purpose. I plant my heel right on your toe. Then, in a rush of conscience, I say, "I'm sorry. I'm really, really sorry (groveling now)."

With enough groveling, you eventually remit and say "That's okay." See what happened? "Isn't it really, really (groveling) too bad what just now happened?" "Yes, it is." There was no admission of guilt on my part, just groveling and weaseling you into saying it was okay.

We can do better than this.

When you are angry and you step on someone's toe, you must use the following words to measure your admission of guilt: "I stepped on your toe. That was wrong. Will you forgive me?"

I can almost guarantee that you cannot say "Will you forgive me?" while you are still angry. Why? Because it requires that you put yourself in a vulnerable position. When you say, "Will you forgive me?" you are subjecting yourself to their mercy. The person offering you forgiveness can say "No." Only a person who has his or her anger under control can ask for forgiveness. It is at that point that an angry person has exerted mental discipline over his or her emotions.

The measure of control that a person has over his or her anger is his or her ability to roll back the time at which he or she can genuinely ask for forgiveness further up the side of the volcano—closer and closer to the point of the explosion. A person who is master of his or her anger is a person who can regularly and reliably listen to his or her conscience when it says, "You are out of line," in the midst of an angry outburst and then immediately ask for forgiveness.

Many years ago, I gave a talk where I outlined the anger volcano. At the end, a man at the height of his legal career came up to me and said, "I wish you would have told me this 35 years ago. It would have saved me 35 years of marital hell."

"Well 35 years ago, I was a kid and hadn't figured this out," I replied.

He responded, "For 35 years, I've never once apologized to my wife. You see, I never thought I was wrong for the **content** of my anger, but I was a complete jerk in the **form** of my anger. I've got to go home and try to make it right."

Have I reached success in controlling anger? Heck no. I wish. I am working along with you on this one. The closer and closer I get to Aristotle's ideal type of anger, the more successful I am. As long as I am battling for this, I think I am succeeding. When I stop trying, then I am failing. My kids can attest to this. Just because I know the right answer doesn't mean it is easy to achieve the right behavior.

Forget about a world where anger doesn't exist. Remember that controlling it on the tail end is the only reliable way of controlling your anger.

Mental Monkey

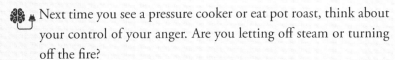 Next time you see a pressure cooker or eat pot roast, think about your control of your anger. Are you letting off steam or turning off the fire?

Next time you are chopping firewood or hitting a bucket of balls at the range or at the batting cages, remember, *perfectly controlled productive, explosive physical activity* can control the chemical consequence of your anger. Hit for accuracy, not distance.

Next time you are shopping at the grocery store and see organically grown pepper, think about PC-PEPA.

Next time you are scolding one of your kids or an employee, remember to differentiate the *form* from the *content* of your anger.

When you are in the midst of an argument with a loved one and the phone rings, ask yourself, "Will I fail the telephone test"?

When you see a hole in drywall or a new remote control on the store shelf, remind yourself that the person who put the hole there or broke the original remote in anger decided to do it. No one loses his or her temper. They decide to misplace it.

Next time you say, "I'm sorry," remember that it only means "Isn't it too bad what just now happened."

Next time you see a volcano, even if only in a picture, remember that the cooldown is the only way to control anger.

The Magic Act (Write This Down)

What **one** thing did I learn in this chapter that I can start applying now?

_____

_____

_____

_____

_____

_____

_____

_____

What **bad habit** of thinking do I want to change after reading this chapter?

_____

_____

_____

_____

_____

_____

_____

_____

_____

_____

What thing in my life will be my "**Mental Monkey**" (my reminder) that will help me to change my thinking from what I learned in this chapter?

_____

_____

_____

_____

_____

_____

What reminders have I posted lately to remind myself to stay on the correct path?

_____

_____

_____

_____

_____

_____

_____

References

Bohart, A.C. (1980). Toward a cognitive theory of catharsis. *Psychotherapy: Theory, Research & Practice, 17*(2), 192.

Bushman, B.J. (2002). Does venting anger feed or extinguish the flame? Catharsis, rumination, distraction, anger, and aggressive responding. *Personality and Social Psychology Bulletin, 28*(6), 724-731.

Crisp, R. (Ed.). (2014). *Aristotle: Nicomachean Ethics.* Cambridge University Press.

Panati, C. (2016). *Panati's Extraordinary Origins of Everyday Things.* Chartwell Books.

SLIPPING ON A BANANA PEEL

A story that illustrates the **actor-observer effect**, how **attribution errors** work, and the **global negative** way that unhappy people view themselves. It can help you understand why some people criticize themselves mercilessly.

What in the Heck Is an *Attribution*?

People like to have a reason for everything. After any disaster (natural or otherwise), we sit in diners and breakrooms trying to figure out why the bad thing happened. A tornado blows through another trailer park in Oklahoma, and people all over the country are jawing about why tornadoes keep making kindling out of manufactured homes. Psychologists say the wizened truck driver who shares his opinion on the matter with his waitress is making an **attribution**. (Actually, we'd say that whenever *anyone* comes up with a reason for anything, they are making an attribution. It doesn't have to be a truck driver.)

In the subfield of social psychology, there has been a long series of experiments examining a certain kind of attribution called the **actor-observer effect**. The actor-observer effect is the difference in attributions (the explanations for an action) of those who are doing something (as the actor) and those who are watching someone else do something (as the observer)—thus, the name. The actor-observer effect is also called the **fundamental attribution error** because it is an error so commonly practiced that it is nearly universal, or fundamental.

Football and the Actor-Observer Effect

There is nothing particularly rare about the actor-observer effect; people do it all the time. For example, on any given Saturday or Sunday in autumn, men and women engage in the actor-observer effect from the comfort of their armchairs while watching football.

Imagine you are at home sitting in your La-Z-Boy, a bag of Doritos on your lap and your favorite beverage within reach. During the game, on a first down, a wide receiver runs downfield. No one is guarding him and he stops—he's not even in motion, standing still near the sideline. It's like he's in the fourth-grade peewee league. He's standing and waiting, waving his arms, and yelling, "Throw it to me! Throw it to me!" The quarterback throws him a cream-puff pass. It's a perfect spiral—not too hard and not too soft. Like Baby Bear's bed, it's just right. It hits the wide receiver (we'll call him Mike) right on the numbers.

Mike drops the ball. On the second down, he runs the same route for the same play: there's no coverage, he's still wide open, and he's standing and waving his arms. The same perfect Baby Bear's bed pass is thrown by the quarterback.

Mike drops it. On the third down, it's the same play, same route, and same ideal Baby Bear pass. The wide receiver is wide open and standing still, yet Mike again drops the ball.

At this moment, you in your La-Z-Boy have a reaction. You stand up, spilling your Doritos (to the delight of your dog), and yell at the TV: "You stink! You're overrated! Get off the field, you bum! My mother can play better than you! You aren't worth $32 million! *You stink! Loser!!*"[5]

This, my friends, is an attribution. It is a specific kind of attribution called a **dispositional** or **characterological attribution**. According to you (the observer), Mike keeps dropping the ball because he has a deeply engrained character flaw that keeps him from catching the ball. Mike is a *loser!* Mike's character is at fault—it's an unchanging, immutable characteristic of the man.

---

5. If you don't know the rules to American football, this is an important point in the action. If you were a fan, you would react the same way.

The explanation for his behavior is that it is characteristic of who he *is*. He drops the ball because he has a ball-dropping disposition. He probably drops everything. He's chronically clumsy, butter-fingered, a complete klutz. And we don't stop at football. Mike is a bad person. He is unworthy of love and deserving of punishment. The *observer* of the behavior usually makes dispositional or characterological attributions.

Now the game is over and the sports reporter shoulders his way through the crowd to Mike and says, "Mike, what happened?"

You never hear Mike say, "I stink! I'm not worth $32 million. I bet your mother could play better than me. I'm overrated! I am a *loser*!"

Instead, Mike probably answers with something like this: "I didn't have my head in the game today. I didn't come to play. I didn't give 110 percent and it showed."

Or he might say, "I have the flu. You may not have seen it, but I've been throwing up on the sidelines throughout the whole game."

Or he says, "I cracked a rib in practice this week and the cornerback kept hitting me in the ribs. In the second quarter, I could feel another one crack, but I kept on playing. I told the coach, but he told me I was the only one who could outrun the cornerback, so I stayed in the game."

Another possible explanation might be, "I got poked in the eye and couldn't see."

These are situation-specific attributions. Why does Mike use these types of explanations? Because Mike is the actor of the behavior, and the *actors* usually make situation-specific attributions of their poor behavior. Everyone else (observers) says, "He's making excuses. Just like a *loser*!"

Negative attributions about others' behavior tend to be characterological rather than situation specific. "He did the thing because that is the kind of person he is." Negative attributions about self tend to be situation specific and not related to stable traits. "I did the thing because of the situation, not because of the type of person I am."

Can a Banana Peel Reverse the Fundamental Attribution Error?

Let me ask you a question I have asked hundreds of people: Suppose you are walking down the street one day and you see a guy walking down the other side of the street in the opposite direction. He slips on a banana peel. He steps on it and, zip-bam, he falls on his tail.

Whose fault is it that he slipped and fell?

The actor-observer effect would suggest that you might say that it was the guy's fault because he's clumsy, he's an idiot, or he must have deserved it—it's karma.

The next day, you're walking down the street again, the same guy is walking down the street on the other side of the road, but today the banana peel is on your side of the street. You step on it and slip, zip-bam, and land on your tail.

Whose fault is it?

Based on what we know about the actor-observer effect, we would think that you might say:

"It was because some idiot put it there."

"Because I wasn't watching where I was going."

"I didn't see it."

But you know, when I ask this question of a pessimistic or unhappy person, these are rarely the responses I hear. In fact, they usually say the exact opposite. In the case of the other guy walking down the street, according to the pessimistic or unhappy person, the guy slipped on the banana peel because he wasn't watching where he was going, it was an accident, or it was the fault of the person who dropped the banana peel. These are situation-specific attributions that favor the other person. These attributions give the other person the benefit of the doubt.

In contrast, when unhappy people and pessimists imagine they slip on the banana peel themselves, the attribution is almost always characterological and negative.

"I am a klutz."

"I am so stupid."

"This is just my luck. It figures."

With unhappy or pessimistic people, the actor-observer effect gets twisted around—they do the opposite.

Why Is This?

The reason that unhappy or pessimistic people get this all twisted around is that a more powerful effect is going on that negates and actually reverses the actor-observer effect. Unhappy and pessimistic people tend to be **global** (dispositional) and **negative** in their attributions about themselves. These are cognitive or mental distortions that are associated with unhappiness and pessimism.

If a person is unhappy or pessimistic and experiences a setback or failure, they will make the attribution that it was just their bad luck.

At work, if a pessimistic or unhappy person does a poor job and gets fired, they will say to themself, "I lost my job because I am unemployable. I've never been a good worker. I'm not smart enough and never will be." These are all *global* (dispositional) and overly *negative* statements. If a person tells themself these inaccurate statements, they will only sink into greater and greater despair. Consequently, they will become less and less able to change their actions to do a better job or find a new job.

When people become overly global and negative, they are probably making a cognitive error. In most cases, people are not unemployable and not unworthy of love. This cognitive error needs to be attacked and replaced with a more accurate thought. People who think in globally negative ways need to set up reminder systems (like the signs along the highway that

Tarzan used to remind himself of the turnoff when he cut a new path in the jungle) to remind themselves that they are thinking inaccurately.

People who tend to think overly global and negative need to recognize that in order to start feeling better, they must think better.

They need to attack the cognitive distortion. For example, I've had some former clients write true statements about themselves and put them in a box. When they start going global in their negative attributions about themselves, they are to bring out their emergency pessimism first-aid kit to read the true messages they wrote about themselves. They instead need to think that while they may bear some responsibility for the bad event, there were situational factors that can be changed to prevent it from happening again.

Happy people tend to look for circumstances they can change to place the odds in their favor. Happy people think they have some positive influence over the outcomes.

Unhappy people assume it was all their fault and there is no escape.

These constant reminders and regular argument (disputation) with your own cognitive errors will, with practice, make it easier to think more accurately. Why? Because you are rewiring your brain's physiology. Your brain's neurons will be connecting in ways that make it easier for you to think accurately.

Mental Monkey

Each time you watch a football game and a wide receiver drops a pass, remember the actor-observer effect. Know that when something bad occurs, you may not have had anything to do with it. If, however, you may have been partially or fully responsible for it, you have to remind yourself that you have the capacity to change your situation.

Whenever you hear a football player (or any professional athlete) explain his actions, remind yourself that he'll probably never say, "I stink." In his mind, he's not making excuses; he's making a situation-specific attribution. Then remember how to talk to yourself more accurately. You may even develop some compassion for a coworker who also makes situation-specific attributions.

When you're wasting time on the internet, watching videos of people doing things that get themselves hurt—like jumping off their garage roof into their above-ground pool, only to have the pool collapse and flood their basement—take a moment to think before you say, "What an idiot!" Remind yourself of the fundamental attribution error. Maybe they typically don't do things like take a header off their garage roof.

Next time you see a banana peel, ask yourself, "How do I talk to myself when I do something that turns out badly?"

If you do these things, you'll be on the way to rewiring your brain, growing new neurons to carry the new habits of thought.

By using these natural life events as reminder systems, you will rewire your brain, change your thinking, and change your life.

The Magic Act (Write This Down)

What **one** thing did I learn in this chapter that I can start applying now?

_____

_____

_____

_____

_____

What **bad habit** of thinking do I want to change after reading this chapter?

_____

_____

_____

_____

_____

What thing in my life will be my "**Mental Monkey**" (my reminder) that will help me to change my thinking from what I learned in this chapter?

_____

_____

_____

_____

_____

What good place (like the Angel Waterfall) would I like to go to (in behavior or thought) but I haven't yet done the work to get there?

_____

_____

_____

_____

_____

_____

_____

_____

What reminders am I going to post to help me remember my new habit?

_____

_____

_____

_____

_____

_____

_____

_____

References

Forgas, J.P. (1998). On being happy and mistaken: mood effects on the fundamental attribution error. *Journal of Personality and Social Psychology, 75*(2), 318.

Jones, E.E. & Nisbett, R.E. (1971). *The Actor and the Observer: Divergent Perspectives on the Causes of Behavior.* Morristown.

Malle, B.F. (2006). The actor-observer asymmetry in attribution: a (surprising) meta-analysis. *Psychological Bulletin, 132*(6), 895.

⑫

THE BEST INMATE
ON DEATH ROW

We're talking about the ***contrast effect***—the propensity
people have for comparing themselves to others to evaluate
their worth. Being able to recognize this way of thinking can
help you avoid the same mistakes your parents made
and become a better person.

Accessories and Undercoating

Before we get to inmates on death row, let's talk about buying accessories. Think about the accessories you purchase—ties, socks, belts, earrings,
purses. Now think about how much you would typically spend for each of
those items. Do you have the amount in your head?

Retailers know how much you think is reasonable to pay for these items.
They call those amounts price points. You know certain things should cost
$9.99, other things should cost $19.99, and yet other things should cost
$49.99. Retailers, however, are interested in getting you to pay more for
an item. How are they able to do this?

One way retailers get consumers to purchase items at a higher price point is
to encourage them to buy accessories right after, or in addition to, making
a larger purchase. Men, when you buy a suit, what does the salesperson
immediately ask you? "Do you need a tie to go with that? Do you have a
shirt? How are you holding up on socks?"

"How are you holding up on socks?" What kind of question is that? If you were at the Alamo, Davy Crocket could ask Jim Bowie, "How are you holding up on bullets?" At the Alamo, bullets were crucial and urgent. In almost no case at a clothing store are socks crucial and urgent. No serious person should ever ask that question about socks. I am pretty sure that no one's life has come crashing to a brutal and sudden end because they weren't holding up well on socks.

Ladies, have you ever been in the Ann Taylor dressing room trying to get over the psychological hurdle that the size you want to fit doesn't really fit as well as the next bigger size? Then a perky salesperson peeks over the door (with you in your underwear) and says, "This fun blouse would look fantastic with that skirt! Why don't I just leave it here for you to try on? Okay?" She darts off to find yet another way to upsell you. You're standing there feeling pretty lousy about yourself (there is a huge mirror and you're in your underwear), so you try on the blouse. It makes you feel better about buying the skirt in the bigger size. You don't even look at the price tag on the blouse.

How do they do it? When you do look at the price tag, you say to yourself, "Well, $49.99 is more than I usually spend on a tie, but I am spending $500 on this suit, so what the heck." Ladies, you look at a pair of $49.99 fashion earrings and think, *They'll perfectly complement this $400 suit. Why not?*

The same goes for buying a car. Right at the end of the deal, the salesperson says to you, "You know, we can do a rust-proofing undercoat for $500." You don't really have a price point for undercoating, but you think to yourself, "I'm spending $40,000 on a car; I should at least protect my investment. Yeah, I'll do it." Later you find out you could have gotten it done for $199 elsewhere, but you tell yourself, "It was worth not having to hassle with it. I know the dealer will stand by the work. It was worth the extra $300."

At no other point in your life would you give away $300. Under normal circumstances, you'd never pay $50 for a tie or $50 for fashion earrings. How did they do it? How did the salespeople upsell you? It is called the

contrast effect. Compared to something that costs a lot (a new suit or a new car), that tie or those earrings or that undercoating doesn't seem expensive. We contrast the prices and relative to the big price the little prices seem really small. We throw lots of money at things when we get caught in the contrast effect.

Now to Death Row

Imagine you are a news reporter who is entering death row in a certain prison to interview an inmate who is scheduled to die. In that prison, there are three guys on death row. These guys are sentenced to die for crimes so heinous that at sentencing, life behind bars didn't seem like punishment enough. As you walk through the last security checkpoint and the gate locks behind you, you pull up to the cell of your interviewee, Joe Bob.

Through the course of the interview, Joe Bob pleads his case:

I may be a murderer, but I'm not as bad as these other guys.

You see Billy three cells down? He killed 33 people in 13 states. They called him the Colonial Killer. See, he is a serial killer. It was his goal to kill at least one person in each of the 13 original colonies and transport the dead body to one of the remaining 37 states, by the order of their admission to the union. He was up to Oklahoma when he got caught in a hotel outside the Osage reservation. He's evil. He'd stalk the person for weeks before he'd finally kill them. That boy ain't right. He ought to be here. He's a menace. In fact, he's still planning New Mexico, Arizona, Alaska, and Hawaii. The world will be better off with him dead.

Then there's Ernest across the way. He killed his whole family after he lost in a game of Scrabble. He says he's always had a problem with anger management. Deep-breathing techniques didn't work for him. It was such a mess that if he hadn't spelled out everyone's names in Scrabble tiles, they never would have identified the bodies. He's even more evil than Billy.

Me, I just killed a gas station attendant. It wasn't really my fault. The guy shouldn't have fought me over the 20 bucks in the register. He wasn't anybody anyway. I hear no one came to his funeral except a preacher who read about it in the newspaper. I really shouldn't be on death row. I had a bad attorney. It's all politics. There's a guy in cell block C that did the same thing as me, and he got life. I'm appealing my case.

And do you know what that makes Joe Bob?

That makes him the best inmate on death row.

I'll bet his mother is proud. I can hear her bragging to all her bingo buddies. "My little Joe Bob isn't like all those other murderers; he's just got a little anger management problem. The therapist is working with him on deep breathing. I think it's helping."

What is it that Joe Bob is doing? He's comparing himself to even more violent criminals and rationalizing his behavior—compared to those guys, he's not so bad. Compared to the suit, the tie wasn't expensive.

Outside of Prison Again

Several years ago, Todd Snider released a song called "Alright Guy." I love the song. The lyrics illustrate the contrast effect perfectly. Give it a listen. In it, he compares his drunkenness and partying to the acts of a serial killer, and what do you know: he realizes he's an "Alright Guy."

The song is very funny (to me) and points out the same cognitive error demonstrated by the death row inmate—contrasting yourself with someone much worse than you. Woohoo! Todd Snider doesn't have a bunch of dead bodies in the trunk of his car, so relatively speaking, getting wild and getting drunk doesn't seem so bad.

And do you know what? He's right. But he's making the wrong comparison. People constantly tell me, "At least I'm not as bad as my old man," or "At least I'm better than my mom ever was." You know what I tell them? (Remember, I scored poorly on compassion in psychology school.)

I tell them, "Big deal. Yippee, you're better than scum." I tell them they have the "Hitler plus one" problem. I'll bet you're better than Hitler, too. And what does that make you? One better than Hitler?

Hitler plus one.

Woohoo! So that makes you as good as who? Goering? Goebbels? Himmler?

Find a *Better* Role Model

I tell people when they make these types of contrasts and comparisons (and it is natural that we make comparisons) that it is more helpful to compare yourself to an aspirational goal rather than to someone you do not want to be like. Why? Because if you are the best inmate on death row, you don't have to make many improvements. Being better than a bad person isn't a very high hurdle. Snails can jump that hurdle. If you compare yourself to the kindest, noblest person you know, then you have lots of improvements to make. You have an aspirational goal to work toward. You have a target to aim for that's worth the effort. If you look to a model to imitate, you can improve yourself.

If you have a model to avoid, you teach yourself how easy it is to be smug.

Invariably, if you compare yourself to losers, you end up making the same mistakes. If you had lousy parents and you tell yourself, "My old man used to beat me. I'll never beat my kids," congratulations; when you avoid beating your kids, you are one better than your dad (buzzer sounds).

You failed to notice that he also called you names, got drunk on a regular basis, and left home for long periods of time. You do the same, but so long as you don't lift a finger to hit your kids, you are a hero in your own mind. Smug and completely deceived.

If you were to choose a model parent to imitate instead, you would know what you want to look like, not what you don't want to look like.

*If you compare yourself to an excellent model, you are
more likely to reach your goal than if you compare
yourself to someone you don't respect.*

Poker-Playing Dogs and the Contrast Effect

When I was in high school, I spent a great deal of time in art class. I loved
art class. I had a great art teacher. Not once did she ever bring in a photo of
dogs playing poker and say, "Do better than this." She brought in photos
of works by Rembrandt, Michelangelo, Monet, Cassatt, Rodin, da Vinci,
and the like. She said, "Imitate these."

I must admit that I am still not a better painter than the guy who painted
the poker-playing dogs. In fact, I would love to be as skilled as the guy
who puts Elvis on black velvet. I guarantee, though, that I am a better
artist having tried to imitate the masters and failed than I ever would have
been if I had compared myself to bad artists.

If you want to be a great man or woman, find role models of people you
want to imitate, not people you can easily surpass.

Mental Monkey

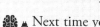 Next time you see Elvis on velvet or a painting of dogs playing poker, remind yourself that these are not your aspirational goals. You want to imitate the best. Ask yourself, "Am I the best inmate on death row?" or, "Am I Hitler plus one?"

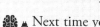 Next time you buy a tie or earrings or undercoating for your car, remind yourself how easy it is to get in the model of thinking, *I'm not so bad.*

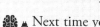 Next time you see a story about a death row inmate, remind yourself that no one gets a prize for being the best inmate on death row. Instead, look to the best in our world and try to be like them.

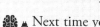 Find a copy of "Alright Guy" and give it a listen (it is a really good song). Hum it to yourself when you are feeling self-satisfied and smug.

Keep at this and you'll change the neurons in your brain that allow you to be smug about being better than the worst. You will grow neurons to be on the lookout for the great people in life, and by imitation, you'll become more like them.

The Magic Act (Write This Down)

What **one** thing did I learn in this chapter that I can start applying now?

_____

_____

_____

_____

What **bad habit** of thinking do I want to change after reading this chapter?

_____

_____

_____

_____

_____

_____

_____

_____

What thing in my life will be my "**Mental Monkey**" (my reminder) that will help me to change my thinking from what I learned in this chapter?

_____

_____

_____

_____

_____

_____

_____

_____

What good place (like the Angel Waterfall) would I like to go to (in behavior or thought) but I haven't yet done the work to get there?

_____

_____

_____

_____

_____

_____

_____

_____

What reminders am I going to post to help me remember my new habit?

_____

_____

_____

_____

_____

_____

_____

_____

References

Cialdini, R.B. (1993). *Influence: Science and Practice*. HarperCollins Publishers.

Cialdini, R.B. (2016). *Pre-Suasion: A Revolutionary Way to Influence and Persuade*. Simon & Schuster.

(13)

BUYING A SLURPEE

How a trip to 7-Eleven can teach us about **addiction** and
relapse prevention—keeping people from slipping
back to problematic addictions.

A Confession

You may not be a priest, but I am about to make a confession. If I win the lottery, I already have my first two purchases lined up. The first thing I'd buy is a pair of socks. Why? Because it would be funny to tell newspaper reporters who ask, "What's the first thing you bought?" I'd get to be a smart aleck and say, "Socks." I guess that tells you a little about the kinds of things that drive me.

The second purchase would be a true extravagance. I would buy a Slurpee machine. You know, the kind that is in every 7-Eleven convenience store in the country. I love a Slurpee on a hot summer day. Shoot, on a bitterly cold winter day, I could be convinced to knock back a Slurpee. Anytime I want one from that day forward, I could pour myself a half-gallon bucket of Slurpee. Is that a little taste of heaven or what? (Okay, maybe it's more like the entrance exam to the college of diabetes.) Maybe this tells you a little more about me than the socks—perhaps more than you wanted to know.

As vices go, Slurpees are not so bad. (But there I go, I'm doing a "Hitler plus one" comparison, right after I taught you how *not* to do that kind of comparison.) We all have bad habits that we'd like to stop. I promise Slurpees will show you the way.

Slurpees as Salvation or Stumbling Block?

Imagine for a moment that you are a recovering drunk with 10 years of sobriety. One day, you're driving home from work, minding your own business, and you see a detour for road construction. No problem. You take the detour, and while you are driving three blocks out of your way, you notice a 7-Eleven in a strip mall by the road. You keep driving.

Every day for a month, you drive by the 7-Eleven as you travel to and from work while the construction is going on. One day, near the end of the construction, you look at the 7-Eleven sign and notice they are selling Slurpees. It is a hot day, so you think, *I could go for a Slurpee.* You pull into the parking lot, walk in, pay with change you found in your center console and under the floor mats, and leave with your frozen ambrosia.

The construction project wraps up and you no longer need to drive the detour route. A couple months later, you are driving home and you think, *Hey, I could go for a Slurpee.* You turn where the detour used to be, stop at the 7-Eleven, and get yourself a Slurpee. Then you drive home.

A couple more months go by. You're driving home and you think, *Slurpee!* You take the detour, pull into the parking lot, plop down your cash, and get yourself a Slurpee. As you are walking out of the 7-Eleven, you look to your right and notice that a couple of shops down from the 7-Eleven, a new sunglasses shop just opened. You think, *I could use some new shades.* Instead of hopping back into your car, you amble down to the sunglasses shop, sipping your Slurpee. You look through the window at the sunglasses and think, *Nah, not now. Mine are fine.* You've been working on your vanity. You jump into your car and drive home.

A couple months later, the Slurpee monster comes calling again, so you do it all again: Buy a Slurpee. Look in the sunglasses shop. Say, "Nah." Drive home.

Two months later, it's the call of the Slurpee again. Slurpee, sunglasses shop, "Nah." This time, however, as you are walking back to your car, you notice a liquor store in between the 7-Eleven and the sunglasses shop. You hop in your car and drive home.

A couple more months go by. Slurpee, sunglasses shop, "Nah," and you look at the liquor store. You say under your breath, "Very bad idea." You get back in your car and drive home.

In a few months . . . Slurpee, sunglasses shop, you look in the liquor store window and think to yourself, *I wonder what those Elvis decanters are going for these days?* (You had a collection in your drinking days. Much to be proud of.) You say to yourself, "Nah, too dangerous."

More time goes by. Slurpee, sunglasses, liquor store. And you ask yourself, "I wonder what Bacardi 151 is going for these days?" (You were, after all, a high-octane rum drinker in your earlier days.) "Oh, what could it hurt?" You go in and look around. You can hear yourself breathe. You're not dizzy, but you are a little off balance. The emotions are intense. You're wandering around a liquor store with a Slurpee in your hand. You are back in familiar territory, but you feel out of place. The helpful clerk with the light-blue apron asks, "May I help you?" "Uh, no." Embarrassed and feeling very guilty, you rush out. You toss the Slurpee in the trash and drive home.

In a few more months . . . Slurpee, sunglasses, liquor store. This time, you go back and the helpful clerk asks again, "May I help you?" You stammer lamely, "Uh, no, just looking." Your conscience yells at you, *What kind of person goes into a liquor store to browse? Is it even possible to window shop for alcohol?*

"Well," the clerk says, "we're having a special on Absolut Vodka." Then you start thinking, *Well, huh. My brother-in-law, Joe, likes Absolut. I think it tastes like boiled potato water. No temptation for me. Maybe it would be nice for me to have some of it around the house for him when he comes to visit. Why should he be punished just because I can't hold my liquor?* Then you mutter, "Nah, what am I thinking?" But on your way out, you check the Bacardi 151 prices. Then you observe, "Rum is immune to inflation."

In a few weeks . . . Slurpee, sunglasses, liquor store. You go in and think, *Well, I'll just look around again. I can handle it. I've already been in here a bunch of times and haven't done anything. I'm cool.* The helpful clerk approaches and this time you notice his badge says, "Brayden." You ask yourself, "With a name like that, can he be old enough to work here?" He says with a voice that has clearly passed puberty, "We're having a special on Bacardi 151." It is like a sign from the heavens. You were meant to buy that alcohol.

You buy it. Back in the car, you pour it in your Slurpee and drink it on the way back home. "Damn, that is good." You ask yourself, "Why have I waited so long?" In short order, your trips to the liquor store become daily and you are back on the path to drunkenness.

Here is my question: When were you in danger of drinking again? What was your first mistake?

The Moment of Truth

I've asked this question of hundreds of people. Some draw the line at the point when the liquor hit your lips. Others take a more extreme view. They say that as soon as you took the construction detour, you were in danger. Others lay the blame on the evils of Slurpees. (Clearly, those people are deluded.) Others lay the blame on sunglasses and vanity. I like a good pair of sunglasses. I don't point the finger there. Slurpees and sunglasses don't make drunks fall off the wagon.

Here's what I think . . .

You were in danger when you walked past the liquor store without noticing it. You should have known you were *already* well on the way to danger when you first noticed it and thought, *I didn't remember this being here last time*. Something must have been going on in your head to delude you into thinking you innocently missed a liquor store. Drunks in recovery don't miss liquor stores, drive-thrus, or the beer aisle at the grocery store. The pink aisle at the toy store is less visible to a 7-year-old girl than a liquor store to a drunk. If you missed it, you were already in danger.

This brings us to the principle: If you have a behavior in your life that is problematic, some habit that causes you grief, you don't *plan* to return to that behavior. If you are a recovering drunk, you don't plan to get drunk while you are eating your Cheerios. Instead, you make thousands of *apparently irrelevant decisions* that make it more likely that you will engage in the problem behavior (Marlatt & George, 1984). You usually talk yourself into it without noticing the one stupid action that is the end of a chain of perhaps a thousand small decisions that led you there.

It's not a conscious decision to do something stupid, and it doesn't just happen. So, by the time you were in the liquor store, you were already careening down the proverbial slippery slope.

When something related to a problem behavior jumps out at you and you realize that you didn't notice it before, you are at that moment already in great danger. *Run away!*

G. Alan Marlatt, a leading researcher in the field of relapse prevention, has written extensively about a model of keeping yourself out of trouble. I recommend reading his works if this topic interests you. Marlatt came up with the term **apparently irrelevant decisions**. His work shows how people with all sorts of problem habits make thousands of tiny little decisions that get them back into trouble.

If you want to enact a do-it-yourself brain repair and rewire your bad habits, you must dissect the thousand apparently irrelevant decisions you make that lead you toward the bad habit. I don't care if the bad habit is drinking, smoking crack, shoplifting, nail-biting, or acting grouchy, you must figure out the thousand little decisions that make it easier or harder to do that behavior.

Slurpee, Sunglasses, Liquor Store Redux

So how exactly do you keep from relapsing? Let's hit the rewind button and start the Slurpee story again. Not when you were digging around in the center console for enough quarters for your first Slurpee. Not even when, on your third or fourth trip, you wander over to look at sunglasses. It was when walking back from the sunglasses shop to your car that you first noticed the liquor store. When you hop back in your car and drive home, the vision of the liquor store is rolling around in the back of your head like static on the AM radio. It is at that point you tell yourself, "How in the world did I miss that? I gotta go talk to my sponsor." In the instant you hear the dog that didn't bark, you know you need help.

You call your sponsor, grab a coffee, and sort out what was clouding your vision. You and your friend figure out the other dozen 7-Elevens in your city that are nowhere near a liquor store. You and your friend, once you've mapped out five new routes home from work, go buy yourself some reward sunglasses.

Every time you change a little thought or little habit,
you are rewiring your brain for success.

Mental Monkey

Next time you see or drink a Slurpee, reexamine the things you are doing to protect yourself from returning to a bad habit. As the nectar of the gods is swirling around in your mouth, mull over what thing has recently jumped out at you as an early warning signal that you are in trouble and you need to *run away!*

The next time you try on a pair of sunglasses, remind yourself that a good pair of sunglasses won't lead you to ruin, but they may distract you from your real temptation.

The next time you see a detour sign, remind yourself that the little decisions in life can take you closer to or further away from self-destructive behavior.

The Magic Act (Write This Down)

What **one** thing did I learn in this chapter that I can start applying now?

_____

_____

_____

_____

_____

_____

_____

_____

_____

What habit in my life is a bad destination (like the Crocodile Swamp) that I'd rather not go to but is easy to do so because I have done it so much?

_____

_____

_____

_____

_____

_____

_____

What thing in my life will be my "**Mental Monkey**" (my reminder) that will help me to change my thinking from what I learned in this chapter?

_____

_____

_____

_____

_____

_____

_____

_____

What good place (like the Angel Waterfall) would I like to go to (in behavior or thought) but I haven't yet done the work to get there?

_____

_____

_____

_____

_____

_____

_____

_____

What reminders am I going to post to help me remember my new habit?

_____

_____

_____

_____

_____

_____

_____

_____

References

Daley, D.C. & Marlatt, G.A. 2006. *Overcoming Your Alcohol or Drug Problem*, 2nd edition. New York: Oxford University Press.

Marlatt, G.A. & Donovan, D.M. (Eds.). (2005). *Relapse Prevention: Maintenance Strategies in the Treatment of Addictive Behaviors.* Guilford Press.

Marlatt, G.A. & George, W.H. (1984). Relapse prevention: Introduction and overview of the model. *British Journal of Addiction*, *79*(4), 261-273.

Marlatt, G.A. & Romaine, D.S. (2008). *The Complete Idiot's Guide to Changing Old Habits for Good.* New York: Penguin Group.

$$\textcircled{14}$$

MATH GENIUSES LIVING IN CARDBOARD BOXES

Catastrophic thinking can distract you into creating a panic situation in your head, making it impossible for you to perform well. Understanding this can help you steer toward solutions instead of staying in misery.

Making a Buck

I went to graduate school at a university that, at the time, had an open admissions policy for undergraduates. This meant that if a student graduated from an accredited high school in the state, the university was obligated to take them. This led to a very high flunkout rate. A university flunking many taxpayers' children is not good for public relations. I paid my way through grad school by teaching. Many of my classmates taught Psychology 100. I didn't. I taught a much different class. It was called *The Psychology of Academic and Personal Effectiveness*. That was a really fancy name for study skills. The class was not populated by your average students. They were typically well below average. Sure, occasionally we'd get a straight-A student slumming for an easy A, but a majority of the students in the class were told by their academic advisors to (a) take the class or (b) leave the university. Some of these students were not the brightest bulbs in the box. Some were having trouble for other reasons altogether. Our course was designed to help retain these students, some of which probably shouldn't have been retained.

Teaching was a challenge. I had one student, a seven-foot-tall guy who would consistently fall asleep in the front row. This student, who was all elbows and knees, would saw logs while I was trying to motivate unmotivated students for success. It was a tough crowd.

I taught one section on test anxiety. Some of these students knew the material but would choke on the exams. I'd ask, "What are the thoughts that go through your head when you are taking a test?" I was surprised at one response—it wasn't the most typical response but one that I still heard so many times I realized it was pretty common. You've got to be a math genius to think like this in the middle of an exam, and the next section explains the thought process.

Math Geniuses

When I take a test, my strategy is to go through the test and answer every question that I know and then add up the score. Then I go back through and answer every question that I am 75 percent sure of. I take that number of questions, multiply by 0.75, and add that to my total. I go through again and answer every question I am 50 percent sure of. I take that number, multiply by 0.5, and add that to my total. Then I go through again with the questions I am only 25 percent sure of, total that number, multiply it by 0.25, and add that result to my score. Then only my totally clueless guesses are left. That is when the tension mounts. You see, I'll be looking at question 17, for instance, and have absolutely no clue about the answer. Then I say to myself, "If I guess right, I'll get 85 percent on this test."

I'll add the 85 percent to the grade I've already computed for this class and realize that I am going to get a B- in the class. I figure that into my grade point average and conclude that I'll have a 2.0 GPA for the quarter. I feel good.

(By the way, who has time for this kind of computation during a test? I was always busy enough just trying to finish my exam!)

But then I think, *If I guess wrong, I'll get 82 percent on the test.* I'll then add the 82 percent to my grade I've already computed for this class and figure that I am going to get a C+ in the class. I figure that into my grade point average for the quarter and realize that I am going to get a 1.9 GPA for the quarter.

You see, I have scholarships and grants that are based on maintaining a 2.0 GPA. I can't pay for school without those scholarships and grants. When I left for college, my dad told me that I better make it work because he wasn't going to throw good money after bad. His last words to me were, "You're on your own now." So if I don't keep these scholarships and grants, I won't be able to pay for school. I live in the dorms, and I can't afford to pay to live there. I don't have a job. I don't have a degree, so I can't get a good job. If I lose my scholarships and grants, they'll kick me out of school. They'll kick me out of the dorm. I won't have a job, I can't go home, and I'll be living on the street in a cardboard box over a manhole cover, drinking Mad Dog 20/20 out of a paper sack.

"You actually think that every time you take a test? Man, if I thought like that, I'd have test anxiety." For bad students about to flunk out of college, these people were remarkable at arithmetic.

The student would laugh and say, "Well, except for drinking liquor out of a paper sack, yeah, that is pretty much what runs through my head."

I guess it beats "living in a van, down by the river"!

Disaster in a Box

When we let our thoughts spiral downward like that toward disaster, we fall into the trap of **catastrophic thinking**. Fear and anxiety quickly blossom, take hold of our thinking, and work to immobilize us. This is particularly problematic because it is such a common tendency that it reinforces itself with regularity, quickly becoming a mental habit. Here's how it works. The person who is living with the fear is troubleshooting the potential problems that could come down the pike. This is about

50 percent of the battle. The other 50 percent, which includes the ability to think of all the other options that could prevent the catastrophe, gets shut off in catastrophic thinking. Catastrophic thinking is malignant advance planning.

Catastrophic thinking creates blinders that prevent us from seeing any potential solution that could stop the disaster from occurring, and it focuses our attention instead on the impending train wreck.

The test-taking student, in the middle of the thoughts racing toward the cliff, never thought, *Hey, maybe they could put me on probation and I could stay in school* or *I heard they have a work-study program for students. Maybe I could get a job* or *Maybe I'll start looking for a job, live tight for a while, and re-enroll next quarter.* Or, *Maybe my dad would take me back in.* Here's another one they never thought of: *Maybe my computations were wrong and I am doing better than I thought.*

In moments of fear or high stress, a person's attention narrows down to a single point. Think, for example, of a race car driver. He must focus only on what is happening on the track. If his attention wanders—"Hey, look at that fat guy in the stands with my number painted on his gut!"—he crashes. To survive, he must focus on the track and the other cars, not the half-naked body-painted fans in the stands. The same occurs with anxiety. Your brain is telling you that you are under threat, and your attention narrows. In this case, it prematurely tells you that you are in danger, and the narrowed focus limits you from thinking of alternate solutions.

If you think like this, your particular malady is pessimism. There are two professions that reward pessimism: lawyers and engineers. Unlike most other professionals, they get paid to find and predict when disaster will occur. Engineers get paid to find and predict failure in things. How will this bridge fall down? What will happen when this car crashes? When a bad thing occurs, what will happen and how do we design around it? Attorneys are trained to do the exact same thing with situations.

Let's say I call up a buddy of mine who is an attorney and say, "I'm picking you up for lunch. Do you think I can double-park out in front of your office?"

He responds, "Yeah, you can if you want, but if they hook you, even if they don't tow you, it will cost $75. If they tow you and the vehicle is damaged, you can be liable for that damage. Your insurance company might not pay for it, so it could be like $3,000 out of your pocket. So double-park if you want."

"Never mind, I'll circle the block." Lawyers are trained to predict how someone is going to get sued or how some bad thing can occur. Their default thinking is to create sequences of events that go from bad to worse and always end with *the worst possible* outcome.

If this is the way you think, even if you aren't a lawyer or engineer, you *are* a pessimist.

You are reading this murmuring under your breath, "I'm not a pessimist. I'm a realist." By the way, what's the difference between a pessimist and a realist? Nothing. There's absolutely no difference between a pessimist and a realist. Pessimists are more realistic than optimists. They can make better predictions about the future than optimists. If you have an optimist and a pessimist predicting the likelihood of an event occurring or not occurring, who's right? The pessimist (Seligman, *Learned Optimism*, p. 109).

Now you might be thinking to yourself, why would I not want to be a pessimist? This is a good gig for me. Here's why: because optimists live longer, happier, healthier lives with more friends. It's your call. Do you want to live a longer, happier, healthier life with more friends, or do you want to be right more often? I'm not talking about the kind of living-in-a-fantasy-world kind of optimist. I'm talking about a particular type of optimist. So let's talk some more about this.

The Three *P*'s of Pessimism

There are three cognitive attribution errors that pessimists make:

- Permanence

- Pervasiveness

- Personalization

First, when a negative event occurs, pessimists think it's **permanent**. When something bad happens, it's going to always happen. Let's imagine I go out with my friends. We're out on the floor dancing, when someone looks at me and says, "Roger, you can't dance. Go sit down. Don't embarrass yourself." So, I go sit down. I'm over by the punch bowl. I have a drink and start telling myself, "I'm no good at dancing. I've never been any good at dancing. I have a bad-dancing gene. I come from a long line of bad dancers. I've taken all of the courses—Fred Astaire, Arthur Murray—it doesn't matter. I even bought the DVDs and cut out the footprints and taped them to the floor. I'll never be a good dancer. I suck at dancing." That's the way a pessimist thinks. Once the bad thing occurs, it will always occur.

After getting a bad grade on a test at school, the pessimist might think, *I'm not good at this class. I've never been good at this class. I'll never be good at this.* If a pessimist has a bad day at work and misses a deadline, they'll say to themselves, "I'm a bad worker. I've always been a bad worker. I'll never be a good worker." That's permanence.

The second error in the way pessimists think is to go universal when a negative event occurs. They take one specific event and expand it to be permanent. Then they expand it to fill the universe. "I suck at everything." That's the **pervasive** attribution. Picture me sitting by myself back at the club. I start thinking, *Not only am I a bad dancer. I can't read music. I can't play an instrument. I don't really have any big talent. I'm not very much fun at parties. Look at me. I'm sitting here by myself. Last week a dog bit me. Kids in the neighborhood pointed and laughed. I suck. I'm a loser. I'm a loser in every area of my life. I am a loser!*

That's the way pessimists think: *Not only am I bad at this, I'm bad at everything, and I'll always be bad at everything. I'm a loser.*

The third cognitive error pessimists make is **personalization**. Personalization is where you say bad things specifically happen to you. Like Eeyore in Winnie the Pooh, you have your own special black cloud that follows you around and rains on you all day long. You feel like Zeus on Mount Olympus has lightning bolts with your name on them.

Do you ever line race at the grocery store? You know what line racing is. You get in the checkout line and you mark yourself with a guy three lanes down. You think, *Oh buddy! I'm going to smoke you today.* You get ready. You loosen up. Only one person is in front of you. Boom. The gate opens. They put the little marker down on the conveyer belt and you start unloading your stuff. *I'm going to make time. I'm going to beat this guy. I am in the fast lane.*

Then the person in front of you says, "I've got coupons," and he pulls out this ball of crumpled up coupons. The clerk uncrumples them to scan but then must type in the numbers because the bar code is messed up. Then you hear, "This one has expired."

"Oh no, you won't take it anyway?" You roll your eyes. Steam builds inside your head.

Sometimes you get behind a person who is buying alcohol, but there's a 14-year-old on the register. Into the microphone, the checker says, "We have a 21 on register four." The manager has to come over, clock in, scan the bottle, and clock out. At some point you wonder, "Oh really. I can't just do that myself?"

The coupons or the alcohol have finally been scanned and you are losing time. You think, *This only happens to me.* Then the customer says, "I've got to write a check." You think, *Why does this* always *happen to me?*

You are driving down the highway and you get behind a grandma in the fast lane. "Why does this always happen to me?" That's personalization.

Pessimists tend to personalize everything. They think **permanent, pervasive,** and **personalized** when bad things happen.

Optimists flip it. So if I'm an optimist and I'm dancing and somebody says, "Roger, you suck at dancing. Go sit down. You're embarrassing yourself." I say, "I don't have my mojo tonight. I don't have my groove on. Next week I'm going to have it back." Instead of thinking my dancing problem is **permanent**, I think it's **temporary**. It's "Give me time and you'll see, I really can dance."

Then if they say, "You suck at dancing, Roger. Stop it. You're embarrassing yourself." What I say is, "I may not be good at dancing, but I'm good at so many other things. It's okay. Even superheroes have their weakness. Dancing is my kryptonite." I think my weakness may be permanent, but it certainly isn't **pervasive**. My weakness is **situation-specific**.

When things go badly at the checkout line, I say, "Hey. I guess today's not my day. I usually am in the fast lane. I can usually determine who is the speedy checker. Next time, I need to get better at identifying the slow customer. I can do that." Rather than thinking Zeus has a slow lane lightning bolt set aside for me and **personalize** it, I see the problems as **external** to me and I can learn to maneuver around them.

Those are the fundamental differences between optimists and pessimists. If you will monitor your thinking and if you typically think **permanently, pervasively** and **personalized** when things go bad, you're probably a pessimist. You will be a happier person if you discipline those thoughts. You can change your thinking if something goes badly to **temporary, situation-specific,** and **external,** and you will become happier as a result. You may not be as naturally ebullient as someone else, but you can be happier than you are today.

The Cure

The only way to get past catastrophic thinking is to practice thinking of alternate solutions. Practice, practice, practice. When you notice that your mind is racing headlong to an impending disaster, put the brakes on and tell yourself, "There are other solutions." Stop and write down as many other solutions as possible. You may need to enlist the aid of a close friend to help you come up with other solutions. Why? Because your anxious brain is narrowing its field of vision to a tight spot of disaster.

If you want to get past this, you need to set up mental markers that remind you that you are getting irrational. (Remember Tarzan's signs to remind him to turn onto the new path to the waterfall?) With practice, you will carve new paths in your brain that will allow you to think differently. In time, you will rewire your brain so you don't run as quickly down the path to disaster.

What do these mental markers look like? Notice your phrases like, "This will never work" or "Just my luck" or "Why does this always happen to me?" Remember the three *P*'s of pessimism: permanent, pervasive, and personal. Replace them with temporary, situation specific, and external to me.

Mental Monkey

 Next time you dream where you are in a class where the instructor is passing out the final exam and you haven't been to school the entire term (by the way, almost everyone has this dream; you are not alone in this one), wake up and tell yourself there are always solutions. You have to stop and remind yourself that there are other options.

 When you are online looking up the top 10 funniest *Saturday Night Live* sketches and you see Chris Farley playing the motivational speaker Matt Foley, remember that you probably won't have to live in a van down by the river.

 Next time you see a NASCAR crash, remind yourself that the driver needs to focus on just one thing. In much of real life, success comes from being able to see alternative solutions. If you get your shorts in a twist about every little thing, you won't be able to see alternative solutions.

 When you are line racing at the grocery store, remember that sometimes you win the race.

 Next time you're out dancing and you see someone who is a bad dancer, remind yourself that he or she is probably very good at lots of other things. When you fail, remind yourself of the same.

 Next time you see Winnie the Pooh, notice Eeyore with his personal black rain cloud and remember personalization.

The Magic Act (Write This Down)

What **one** thing did I learn in this chapter that I can start applying now?

_____

_____

_____

_____

_____

_____

_____

_____

What **bad habit** of thinking do I want to change after reading this chapter?

_____

_____

_____

_____

_____

_____

_____

_____

What thing in my life will be my "**Mental Monkey**" (my reminder) that will help me to change my thinking from what I learned in this chapter?

_____

_____

_____

_____

_____

_____

_____

_____

What good place (like the Angel Waterfall) would I like to go to (in behavior or thought) but I haven't yet done the work to get there?

_____

_____

_____

_____

_____

_____

_____

_____

What reminders am I going to post to help me remember my new habit?

_____

_____

_____

_____

_____

_____

_____

_____

_____

References

Beck, A.T., Emery, G. & Greenberg, R.L. (2005). *Anxiety Disorders and Phobias: A Cognitive Perspective*. Basic Books.

Ingram, R.E. & Kendall, P.C. (1987). The cognitive side of anxiety. *Cognitive Therapy and Research*, *11*(5), 523-536.

Seligman, M.E. (2006). *Learned Optimism: How to Change Your Mind and Your Life*. Vintage.

Vasey, M.W. & Borkovec, T.D. (1992). A catastrophizing assessment of worrisome thoughts. *Cognitive Therapy and Research*, *16*(5), 505-520.

(15)

BUYING TOOTHPASTE

From a simple shopping trip, we can see how prejudice develops. The same **representativeness heuristic** process we use to choose toothpaste and peanut butter leads to prejudicial thinking.

Shopping and Shortcuts

Do you remember the first time you ever went grocery shopping by yourself? I do. I went to a local store called Fazio's. I was living on my own in an efficiency apartment. I had my coupons. I had my list. I was in control. I was excited.

It took forever.

I looked at every item on my list and then looked at every brand for each item. If you do the math, I had only about 20 items on my list, but there were seven to ten different brands for each item on my list. I had a lot of decisions to make.

Consider toothpaste. There I was in the toothpaste aisle in the midst of a Herculean mental debate. *Mom always got Crest with the red triangle. Now that I am calling the shots, I could, if I wanted, get the Crest with the green triangle. Hey, if I want to go wild, I could buy Close-Up. Who's to stop me?* I was mad with power.

I spent about 10 minutes looking at each kind of toothpaste and examining the ingredient list to see if it met my high toothpaste standards. To tell you the truth, I didn't know beans about toothpaste, but I prided myself on making rational decisions. I thought I should read the labels. The old ladies in the store were reading labels, so I thought that was proper grocery store behavior. Heck, if *Consumer Reports* had done a toothpaste rating, I probably would have brought it along. After deciding which brand of toothpaste to buy, then came the mathematical task of computing the price per ounce for each item on my list. This was before the days when the stores put the price per ounce on the shelf. Was it really true that bigger equals cheaper per ounce? Yes, by gum, it was!

I was a sight—a young guy standing in front of the toothpaste display for 15 minutes with a calculator. I looked like I thought I was James Bond solving the mental puzzle that Dr. No had created. "Bond, if you don't solve the puzzle, I will destroy ze vorld in 10 minutes. Ha, Ha, Ha!" This was an important task. I could save three cents.

Choosing peanut butter was also a huge undertaking, but after another 10 minutes and some serious number crunching, I landed on Skippy Super Chunk.

It took me over three hours to find the 20 items on my shopping list. I was proud but mentally exhausted.

Over time, it got easier to go shopping. I'd walk down the peanut butter aisle and pick up the biggest container of Skippy Super Chunk. I didn't even have to look twice. All I had to do was look for the blue lid and the Skippy colors on the label; I didn't have to read the label or the price tag—nothing. Toothpaste became just as easy. Crest, white box, red triangle, and biggest size. Bam. I was done. Shopping took about 20 minutes, and I was the picture of grocery-shopping cool (if that is even possible).

I'll bet many of you have the same sort of rules for shopping. Whatever the rule, whether it is brand or price or big size, it is the same rule each time you go shopping.

You may remember our previous discussion of heuristics in chapter 8 when we talked about Slug Bug (Kahneman and Tversky, 1974). Judgmental heuristics are mental shortcuts that we take in order to get through our day more quickly and allow our brains to work more efficiently. The one in play here is called the **Representativeness Heuristic**—in which a rule you make for one instance is true for all instances of the same thing. My mental shortcut with toothpaste was Crest, big white box, red triangle. If it was Crest in a big white box with a red triangle, it safely represented the kind of toothpaste I wanted. It allowed my brain to work more efficiently and focus on things I would rather do.

Pulling a Fast One

Manufacturers know that consumers do this, so they use this information to increase their profits. (I don't blame them. They have employees who are saving for their kids' orthodontia. Bigger profits mean Christmas bonuses and straighter teeth.) Many people have the mental shortcut that big equals cheaper per ounce. To increase their profits, some manufacturers make the biggest size more expensive per ounce than the small size because they know that many people don't shop price; they use the "big equals cheaper per ounce" representativeness heuristic instead. Once I found that three tiny boxes of Cheerios were cheaper per ounce than one large box. I have children who can each eat a tiny box of Cheerios in one sitting and ask for more, so I typically wouldn't think of buying a small box since it would only last a single meal. In this case, however, it would be the cost-effective choice. The mental shortcut works great until there are added complexities—for example, manufacturers being smart about heuristics.

> *Mental shortcuts help us because they* **usually** *work, but when they don't work, they break in a big way.*

Shopping and Prejudice

Problems develop when we use these mental shortcuts in situations where they are more likely to break down. We use them even when the situation is very complex. The representativeness heuristic of "Skippy equals good" is a pretty safe bet. The representativeness heuristic of "my color of skin equals good" is a much less safe bet. One reason we are prejudiced is that stereotyping is a mental shortcut. Stereotyping is a major factor in prejudice—even if the stereotype is positive.

You may have heard the joke about the European Community. Advocates are saying that it will combine the best of each of the cultures. The British have great customer service and are polite. The French have great food. The Germans build great cars. The Italians make great music. Opponents say, "Oh, so we'll drive our Italian car to the restaurant to eat British food served by a French waiter while listening to German music." That is a nightmare.

Now that I have offended the majority of the European Community, I'll dig the hole a little deeper. We would all agree to stereotypes and laugh— until we meet the stoic Italian or the rude Brit or the garrulous Swede. Then the heuristic stops working. Hmm . . . what are we to do?

Our problem is that we want the stereotype to keep working (because it is efficient and keeps our brains from having to work too hard) when it clearly won't ever approach the complexity of a real person. Our very real problem is that people are eminently more complex than Skippy peanut butter.

As soon as some complexity is factored in, the representativeness heuristic breaks down. The mental shortcut becomes unreliable. Stereotyping allows our brains to work more efficiently so we can spend more time on other things, but it is fairly fallible. We stereotype because it is easier, but that doesn't make it work.

Other Heuristic Stumbling Blocks

Shopping and international relations aren't the only places where the representativeness heuristic breaks down. How many of you have decided to hire an expert because his or her price was the highest? I work with some lawyers, and each can nod their head knowingly about the few attorneys in town who are both wildly expensive and completely incompetent.

Let me give you a more mundane example. I was talking to a guy who was wearing a Rolex. I was wearing a Timex. His watch told time. My watch told time. His watch cost somewhere between $2,000 and $10,000. Mine cost somewhere between $15 and $20. He had owned his watch for five years and had sent it to the shop several times for repairs in the same five years; I had to change the battery in my watch twice in five years. He had bought into the representativeness heuristic that the more expensive the watch, the better it would keep time. But his watch had stopped keeping time several times and cost him several hundred dollars to repair each time. Mine stopped twice because the battery wore out. I went to Walmart and bought a new battery. I was back in business. His representativeness heuristic that "expensive equals high quality" fell apart.

His representativeness heuristic of expensive equals high status still held up though. No one ever looked twice at or was impressed by my Timex.

The same goes for hiring decisions. Very often, we think that when we are hiring an employee, it is easy to say he or she looks and acts the part. When you are evaluating complex behavior like work behavior, however, it is important to evaluate in more complex ways. Are you evaluating the job requirements with a person's job skills? In many cases, people are hired independently of their specific job skills. We very often assume that a person from a good school with lots of brains is a good bet. Ted Kaczynski, the infamous Unabomber, was a Harvard graduate and quite possibly a genius, but clearly, he would not make a solid hire. He is the poster child for the breakdown of this heuristic.

Heuristics are at work in choices for leaders as well. Very often the guy who looks like a leader—tall, lantern jaw, good looking—gets elected over the eminently more qualified short, round woman wearing sensible shoes. Obvious breakdowns of significant representativeness heuristics are now compounded by the fact that our society is becoming so complex that our heuristics about people are breaking down all over the place. We are being forced to think harder about tiny insignificant decisions.

We each have a **daily decision load**—the number of decisions we can make each day before we suffer from **ego depletion** (a.k.a. decision fatigue).

In his book, *Willpower: Rediscovering the Greatest Human Strength*, University of Florida academic psychologist Roy Baumeister defines ego depletion as the lack of cognitive reserve to actively think about a problem. Our brains work a lot like our biceps. Each of us fatigues after doing a certain number of push-ups. Our biceps are out of energy to do any more. When our brains have made too many decisions in a day, we are all out of energy to make any more decisions. It doesn't matter if the decisions are momentous or trivial, they all add up to our **daily decisional load**. After we hit this mark, it's like we can't think anymore. All our mental effort on tiny decisions impairs our ability to reserve mental energy for really important tasks.

Let's go back to the grocery store.

Have you been shopping for peanut butter lately? When I started shopping on my own, there were three kinds of Peanut Butter—Skippy, Jif, and Peter Pan. If you wanted to go wild, you got the chunky kind. Today you can get peanut butter in flavors like double almond mocha cappuccino. What is this, Starbucks? And it's not just peanut butter. One night, I was looking up and down the snack aisle at potato chips. I didn't know if I should get baked, fried, barbeque, sour cream and onion, wild salsa (as opposed to regular salsa), salt and vinegar, pickle, jalapeño, organic (versus the less pure "all natural"), or one kind that actually said on the label, "Could cause anal leakage." At that, I gave up and bought some carrots. (Those last potato chips were wisely taken off the market.)

Why do I bring this up? If we fill our head with a thousand tiny complexities, we use up all our mental effort solving silly little problems rather than the big ones—like how do we get along with people who look and act and believe differently than we do? How do we understand the complexities of cultures, so we don't go killing innocent people just because they wrap their heads in turbans? [6]

---

6. Respectfully remember Balbir Singh Sodhi.

In order to be at our peak mental game, we have to rid ourselves of the thousand tiny decisions so we won't inaccurately use a mental shortcut on a really important decision. It will probably mean doing fewer things and simplifying your life. It will also be the judicious use of habits (which are long behavioral strings of actions) which reduce your cognitive load. (You do this while brushing your teeth. It is a set of complex behaviors that you do not have to think about). The more behavioral habits you have, the fewer decisions you will have to make.

Some famous people (Mark Zuckerberg and Steve Jobs come to mind) have very simple wardrobes, so they can save their decision-making for more important things. In my case, I have black and brown shoes. I have one black and one brown belt. I have only light blue and white dress shirts. I have black and dark grey suits. Why? Because it reduces the number of decisions I have to make when getting dressed. I may someday go as far as Steve Jobs and only wear one color clothes, but I'm not there yet. If it worked for Johnny Cash, it might just work for you.

You can also limit the kinds of foods you eat. When you go to a restaurant, it will certainly reduce the number of options you have on the menu and help you save your decisions for more important things.

Recognizing the role representativeness heuristics can play in creating prejudicial thinking can help you avoid applying stereotypes in more complex situations, especially those concerning people you don't personally know. You want to save your decisions so you can think in a more complex way about people you don't already know. You'll save yourself some headaches and maybe even make the world a little better place.

Mental Monkey

 Next time you are in the store and you look at the little price label under the cereal box, remind yourself that you are resorting to the price representativeness heuristic. As you look up from the shelf and down the aisle at the person with a different color skin, remind yourself that Cheerios are infinitely simpler to understand than that guy. Save your mental effort for understanding that guy.

 The next time you are about to hire someone and you tell yourself, "They are from a good school," stop and think of the Unabomber. Maybe you can keep a jar of Skippy on your desk to remind you how easy it is to resort to the mental shortcut of stereotyping people. If you do, you will eventually rewire your brain to save your mental effort for the really important decisions.

 When you brush your teeth tonight (I'm making a big assumption here), remind yourself that people are harder to understand than the glob on the end of your toothbrush.

The Magic Act (Write This Down)

What **one** thing did I learn in this chapter that I can start applying now?

_____

_____

_____

_____

_____

What **bad habit** of thinking do I want to change after reading this chapter?

_____

_____

_____

_____

_____

_____

_____

What thing in my life will be my "**Mental Monkey**" (my reminder) that will help me to change my thinking from what I learned in this chapter?

_____

_____

_____

_____

_____

_____

_____

What habit in my life is a bad destination (like the Crocodile Swamp) that I'd rather not go to but is easy to do so because I have done it so much?

_____

_____

_____

_____

_____

_____

_____

_____

_____

References

Baumeister, R.F. & Tierney, J. (2012). *Willpower: Rediscovering the Greatest Human Strength*. Penguin.

Johnson, D.K. (2018). Representative Heuristic (chapter 93, pp. 382-384), in *Bad Arguments: 100 of the Most Important Fallacies in Western Philosophy*, Arp, R., Barbone, S. & Bruce, M. (editors). Wiley.

Kahneman, D. (2011). *Thinking, Fast and Slow*. Macmillan.

Kahneman, D., Slovic, S.P., Slovic, P. & Tversky, A. (Eds.). (1982). *Judgment Under Uncertainty: Heuristics and Biases*. Cambridge University Press.

Lewis, M. (2016). *The Undoing Project: A Friendship That Changed the World*. Penguin U.K.

Tversky, A. & Kahneman, D. (1974). Judgment under uncertainty: Heuristics and biases: Biases in judgments reveal some heuristics of thinking under uncertainty. *Science, 185*(4157), 1124-1131.

16

A HORSE NAMED SUKEY

A story that illustrates, with an example from an old Western movie, why people return to the familiar even when something better is available. Understanding this can prevent you from getting into yet another bad relationship, voting for the same bad candidate, or investing your money badly.

One Saturday Afternoon in February

When I was a kid in the 1970s, television was different than it is today. Hop in the way-back machine to an Ohio Saturday afternoon in February. Except for one winter, when we got enough snow to last a lifetime—or so it seemed to my 10-year-old self—I often spent Saturday afternoon indoors looking for something good to watch on television. I'd wear my wide-wale corduroys and my Joe Namath New York Jets sweatshirt and sit in my brown beanbag chair on earth-toned shag carpet in front of a white plastic, Philips black-and-white TV with a bag of taco-flavored Doritos on my stomach.

In those years, we only got four channels: NBC, ABC, CBS, and PBS on a UHF channel with a little fine-tuning on the outside of the channel selector. Sure, I had to fiddle with the antennae, but it eventually came in. For those of you who weren't there, there were no satellite dishes, no cable

TV, no 250 channels, and no internet—so obviously no Netflix, Hulu, or Apple TV. Choices were limited.

So here is the Saturday afternoon lineup in February in the 1970s. On ABC, it was *Wide World of Sports*. In the winter, they'd show lots of winter sports. On a good Saturday, you'd get to see guys jumping barrels on their ice skates. For a preteen boy, it was awesome to watch guys crash into the last of those barrels as they landed. On most Saturdays, however, it was ice dancing. Booorrring! What in the heck is ice dancing? Is ice dancing the "sport" for the less talented ice skaters? Nope. I wasn't watching that.

On CBS, it was the Los Angeles Lakers beating whatever team they were playing. I did like watching Kareem Abdul-Jabbar and his sky hook, but there wasn't really much tension. Those Lakers games were a lot like the third quarter of the Harlem Globetrotters versus the Washington Generals. If you've ever seen the Globetrotters play, you know there is no comedy in the third quarter of those games; just straight lopsided beat-down basketball. So, I got up from the beanbag and changed the station. Remote controls were rare at this point in history.

On PBS, it was opera. 'Nuff said. I wasn't watching that.

All that remained was NBC. On NBC, there was inevitably some old Western you've probably seen. You know the type of movie I'm talking about: Bad guys ride into town (and of course the chief bad guy is wearing the obligatory black hat). They ride around and shoot up the place. They shoot a water barrel and water comes streaming out. Some nebbish guy is hiding behind the barrel and then skedaddles into the bar with the swinging doors banging back and forth. There is always one Mexican guy in the gang. He's wearing the obligatory sombrero and double bandoliers crisscross his chest. A mom with her hair in a bun and her kids are looking out of the bottom of the window in the general store. Sure, you've seen this one. The bad guys rob the bank, shoot some more holes in barrels, and ride out of town. The formula was as ubiquitous as the taco Doritos I was eating.

And since you've already seen this movie, you know there is only one man brave enough to chase the bad guys out of town. It's Jeb (wearing the obligatory white hat), riding on his faithful horse, Sukey. Jeb chases them, firing his six-guns, reins in his teeth, and Sukey in full gallop.

If you've ever fired a pistol, you know it is hard to hit a target. If you've ever ridden a horse at a full gallop, you know that your whole body is being rattled. The thought of firing a revolver at a full gallop and hitting anything other than air is fantasy. Here is where we all suspend our disbelief. You know what happens next, right? Jeb is firing forward, guns a-blazing, and hits a bad guy. You already know who he hits. It's always the Mexican guy. Of course, you knew that. You've seen this movie. Everyone has!

The chief bad guy turns around in his saddle (at a full gallop), fires over his shoulder backward, and hits Jeb. And you already know where he hits Jeb. (It is always a shoulder wound on his non-dominant side—never a gut shot, never a head shot, and never, never the horse). You've seen this movie, right?

Jeb reels back in the saddle and falls to the ground.

Now at this point, I don't care about the bad guys getting away with the loot. I don't care about Jeb lying on the desert canyon floor bleeding from a shoulder wound. What I care about is Sukey. With Jeb bleeding out in the hot, hot sun, what does she do? That's right, you already have seen this movie. She stops, she comes back to Jeb, and she nuzzles him with her nose. Then what does she do? She trots back to the barn.

Later, some old geezer with a scruffy beard and the brim of his hat pinned straight up in front walks into the barn (pulling on his suspenders) and finds Sukey munching hay in her stall. He runs back to the bunkhouse and says, "Sukey's in the barn with her saddle on and all lathered up from a run!"

"Where's Jeb?"

"I don't know."

"Let's round up a posse and find him."

Yes, you've seen this movie.

Now here's my question: Why would Sukey go back to the barn? I mean, here's her life: Some guy straps a big heavy dead animal skin on her back. He puts a cinch around her belly and tightens it as tight as he can. Jeb is no small man. He swings himself right on top of her. The exact same spot on her back that a mountain lion would be in right before it rips at her neck. Yeah, Sukey is not loving this. He puts a metal thing in her mouth that cracks at her back teeth, pokes the roof of her mouth, and yanks her this way and that. And to top it all off, he has these sharp things attached to the heels of his boots that he uses to kick her in her sides. What the heck kind of life is that?

If I were Sukey, I'd leave Jeb in the hot, hot sun. I'd run off and leave him. In fact, I might even step on him as I was going. Maybe a little horsey dance on his head would set things straight. I'd rub up against a rock until that saddle came off and the bit popped out of my mouth. It might take a long time and be painful, but then I could run free with the mustangs. No more spurs in my life.

So why does Sukey go back to the barn?

Because she knows the way.

Sukey knows what happens in the barn. It isn't the best, but it is what Sukey knows. Even though she gets cracked teeth and spur scars, Sukey gets fed in the barn. So she goes back.

People are not that much different from animals. People tend to be just like Sukey. People return to the familiar rather than seeking out what is best.

People Are Just Like Sukey

Many years ago, I heard a story about the liberation of the concentration camps in WWII. Perhaps this is not a true story, but it's vivid, so I retell it. Perhaps you've heard it as well. At the end of WWII, as the allies were liberating the concentration camps, the troops found a man who was in solitary confinement. This man had been alone in a dark box in the basement of a prison. The troops led him up the stairs and into the light of the day, a sight he had not seen for a long time. As the light reached his face, he turned around and went back down the stairs. He walked back to his cell and climbed back into the box.

The change, though good, was uncomfortable. The light was bright, people were scurrying around, and there was a lot of noise. The box was quiet and controlled. The prisoner didn't have to make any decisions. It was familiar.

When I was a teenager, I met with a young man who was only a year older than me and who had just spent 18 months in prison. He was a relative of a family friend. His aunt called my mom and asked me to take him out to lunch—show him some friendship. I can still remember picking him up for lunch. As he climbed into the car, I started babbling about nothing, trying to hide my discomfort. I had never had lunch with an ex-con, and I was nervous.

After a few minutes, I asked him where he wanted to eat. He said, "You decide." I responded, "Hey, you haven't been able to eat at a restaurant for a year and a half. I've been able to do as I pleased. Why don't you decide?" He returned, "That's the thing. For the last 18 months, the prison has decided everything for me. They decided when I would eat, what I would eat, when I'd go to bed, when I'd wake up, when I'd go to the bathroom, when I'd shower, what I'd wear, how fast I'd walk, and everything else I did. I don't know how to make decisions anymore. You decide."

Here he was faced with freedom, and he had forgotten how to decide. In fact, he abdicated deciding. In some ways, he was asking me to take control of his life because it was a familiar circumstance, not because it was best.

Sukey and the Status Quo Bias

What we see in Sukey the horse is what Nobel Prize-winning economist Daniel Kahneman calls the **status quo bias**. Humans (and horses) like things to stay the way they are. If you are prone to the status quo bias, you will see any change as a loss. Kahneman and others have studied this in all kinds of decisions—how to invest your money, which type of car insurance you will choose, which retirement plan you will choose, and whether or not you will donate your organs when you walk into the Department of Motor Vehicles. When scientists looked at the brains of people choosing to walk away from a status quo decision, they concluded that those decisions were more effortful (harder) than sticking with what you already have. In all cases, we tend to stick with the choice we have already made.

Sukey and the Wonderful World of Consumer Goods

The desire to avoid change and return to the status quo isn't just the domain of horses and ex-cons. Every one of us does it when we go shopping. A great deal of research suggests that people tend to evaluate things as better when the things are familiar, even though the thing is not really objectively better (see Madden, 1960 or Gilovich, 1981 for examples).

Let's look at this in real life. Consumer research, specifically research on branding, has studied this tendency and found that once a person is familiar with a brand, he or she will rate an identical product of that brand as better than that of an unfamiliar brand (Park and Lessige, 1981). Companies use this knowledge to sell more products by releasing new products under the brand or trade name of another very familiar product. This is why we have V-8 Juice Splashes that have nothing in common with the thick, red vegetable purée that is V-8. It is why we have Sunkist candy. The only thing the candy has in common with oranges is the color and the name. This is why we have Harley-Davidson brand clothes. I doubt the engineers at Harley-Davidson sit around and design leather vests for the people who ride their motorcycles or are Harley wannabes. It is the familiarity of the name that gets people to buy the new product.

I was friends with a woman who had been an intern at a large consumer products company. She worked on a team that was in charge of the development of a new orange juice. She told me that taste tests showed consumers were going to love this *way* more than any of the other orange juices on the market. As a guy who thinks orange juice is the nectar of the gods, I was looking forward to trying this new juice. I asked her when it was coming out. She said it already did and it was a spectacular flop. No one bought it. Why not? Because no one wanted to take the $1.79 gamble on a new orange juice. They were more than happy to stick with what they knew instead of making a $1.79 mistake. That orange juice does not exist today.

The familiar is seen as better than the new. People's brains are efficiency-seeking machines. That is a nice way to say that we do not like to think. As we discussed earlier, thinking is a taxing process. People avoid it as much as possible—and I don't mean just high school students. To return to the status quo and to avoid change keeps the person from having to solve problems and get the "little gray cells" active. Brain activity is taxing work. We go with what we know.

Horse Sense in Businesses

People are likely to rate the situations they know better than the ones they don't know. When it is election time, people grunt while they pull the lever for the incumbent politicians. "Better the devil we know than the devil we don't know." In my work, I see this all the time. I am in the business of mindset change. I train people and organizations for mindset change. What works for brands and politicians works in companies as well. People resist change initiatives at work because they think, *That's the way we've always done it.*

I spoke to a man who took over a department and found that each day the department printed out one and a half feet of paper with the day's shipping orders. I don't mean a paper one and a half feet long; I mean a stack of paper one and a half feet thick. He asked around to see if anyone ever looked at it. It turns out that some boss ordered it something like 10 years prior; no one had *ever* looked at it since. At the end of each day, that 25 pounds of paper was tossed in the trash.

He asked, "Why do you guys keep printing it out?" Each time, he got back the mantra: "Because that's the way we have always done it." (To his credit, he told them to stop printing it. Tree huggers everywhere rejoice!)

In the same vein, some people stay in jobs that are going nowhere when they have the potential to succeed elsewhere. They never make the move because they are accustomed to their current situation. I have done a great deal of career transition consultation in my work. I work to help people in midcareer figure out how to have more meaning in their lives. I can't tell you how many times I've heard this phrase: "Gee, I'd like to, but we have become accustomed to our current standard of living. I don't think we could make that kind of change."

These are the hopeless words that play off the lips of pale, gray-skinned men who sound like the protagonist in the song "Synchronicity II" by the band The Police. Give the song a listen to hear the world grinding him down because of his status quo bias.

These are miserable people whose marriages lay in shambles. Their kids' lives consist of shuttling in a car from school to soccer practice to gymnastics to bed. They want something different, but they are too afraid to change.

So, like Sukey, they go back to the barn.

Businesses as a whole either change to adapt to the environment, or they die. But people within the businesses often are unwilling to change because it is difficult. They do not realize that if they don't change, the job that has been so stable for so many years may not exist in the next few. If the people in the businesses don't change, the businesses don't change; they cease to exist, the job evaporates, and because the workers weren't willing to undergo a small change, they are forced into the dramatic change of unemployment.

People who are successful in life are able to balance change and stability.

If a woman wants to keep her house and car and lifestyle (stability), she must be willing to change her work habits, her thinking habits at work, or her work location (change). All of this "change" is fundamentally a change in the brain. Any change in a person's environment creates a change in thought habits. Any change in thought habits is never an easy or smooth change. Change your job, and your brain grows new neurons to adapt and learn the new situation. This neurogenesis takes a great deal of caloric energy and is physically tiring. People are literally too tired to change.

Sukey and Wife Beaters

This pattern of returning to the familiar also applies to people in bad relationships. Over and over, I have seen women leave one abusive man only to get attached to another abusive man. Why? Because the abused woman knows how to act in an abusive relationship.

She doesn't know how to interact with a man who is kind and gentle. When he is kind and gentle, she doesn't know what to do. That lack of predictability is hard to live with, so she returns to a man she can predict.

"When he gets angry, at least I know how it will turn out. I don't like how it is going to turn out, but at least I know what the future will hold."

You do what you know—you return to what is familiar, not what is best. She knows what an abusive man looks like, so she returns to what she knows. The abused woman, unless she changes her thinking, will gravitate to another abusive man. With change comes uncertainty. If she gets back with another abusive man, at least she knows how it will turn out. Without the work of rewiring her brain, it is easier to return to what she knows. No new neurons grew to relearn how she might interact with a gentle man.

And, like people who are brand loyal, she will rate the situation she knows as better than the situation she doesn't know. "You know, he's not so bad. He's just misunderstood. At least he pays the bills." Like the blindly loyal brand consumer, she rationalizes her choice (rational lies). Like Sukey, she goes back to the barn.

My understanding of Darwin's theory is that when he was talking about survival of the fittest, he didn't equate *fittest* with *strongest*. He meant that the fittest species was the *one most adaptable to change*. Those who succeed in the world are those who adapt to change the best. Change is hard. We always become habituated to our current situation. In order to have a better life and thrive, we must change our thinking—we must rewire our brains by thinking differently. We need to lay down new neural pathways. The growth of those neurons is physically taxing (and one important reason why babies and children sleep so much).

One of the problems Sukey had was that she didn't know what life would be like outside the barn. If she had a plan, then she might have been more likely to leave Jeb. People are the same; the familiar looks really good when compared to nothing. If you are unhappy with your job or your life, if your business is not changing to adapt to the new environment, then you must have a plan. A plan must have a specific, behavioral, observable, measurable goal and a path to achieve it.

What does a plan look like?

- First, successful people write it out.
- Second, successful people review it regularly.
- Third, successful people include specific, behavioral, observable, measurable outcomes.
- Fourth, successful people are flexible with the outcome. You don't have to do exactly what you plan, but you must at least have a target toward which you aim. "If you aim at the stars and miss, at least you'll hit the moon."

If you can think about what your world could look like if you or your organization changed, then you have a future. If you keep on doing the same thing, you will be stuck in the barn.

Mental Monkey

Next time you watch an old Western and see the horse go back to the barn, remind yourself how we return not to what is best but to what is familiar.

Next time you see any horse, remind yourself that we aren't that much different. We will return to the barn because we know what will happen.

Whenever you buy a product because you know the brand, remember that it is this same thinking habit that keeps you stuck in an unpleasant job or lifestyle. That familiar label on the tub of sour cream doesn't make it objectively better than the other tub. It is just easier.

During the next election cycle, when you are voting for the incumbent and say, "Better the devil you know than the devil you don't know," remind yourself of Sukey.

The next time you hear "Synchronicity II" by The Police playing while you shop, remind yourself that by rewiring your brain, you can escape a soul-crushing life.

The next time you see someone doing something stupid at work because they think, *That's the way we've always done it*, remind yourself that it is within your power to change your thinking and your life.

The next time you hear another news story about an abused woman returning to an abusive relationship, remind yourself that you aren't much different.

When you hear of a business shuttering its doors because it hasn't kept pace with the changing business landscape, remind yourself that you *can* rewire your brain.

The Magic Act (Write This Down)

What **one** thing did I learn in this chapter that I can start applying now?

_____

_____

_____

_____

_____

_____

_____

What **bad habit** of thinking do I want to change after reading this chapter?

_____

_____

_____

_____

_____

_____

_____

What thing in my life will be my "**Mental Monkey**" (my reminder) that will help me to change my thinking from what I learned in this chapter?

_____

_____

_____

_____

_____

_____

_____

_____

_____

References

Fleming, S.M., Thomas, C.L. & Dolan, R.J. (2010). Overcoming status quo bias in the human brain. *Proceedings of the National Academy of Sciences, 107*(13), 6005-6009.

Gilovich, T. (1981). Seeing the past in the present: The effect of associations to familiar events on judgments and decisions. *Journal of Personality & Social Psychology, 40*(5), 797-808.

Kahneman, D. (2011). *Thinking, Fast and Slow.* Macmillan.

Kahneman, D., Knetsch, J.L. & Thaler, R.H. (1991). The endowment effect, loss aversion, and status quo bias: Anomalies. *Journal of Economic Perspectives, 5*(1), 193-206.

Madden, J.M. (1960). Familiarity effects in evaluative judgments. *United States Air Force Wright Air Development Division Technical Note, 61,* 261.

Park, C.W. & Lessig, V.P. (1981). Familiarity and its impact on consumer decision biases and heuristics. *Journal of Consumer Research, 8*(2), 223-230.

Samuelson, W. & Zeckhauser, R. (1988). Status quo bias in decision making. *Journal of Risk and Uncertainty, 1*(1), 7-59.

Conclusion

ONE PIECE AT A TIME

How do you take what you've learned and apply it to your daily life? Together we will map out a simple strategy to make a change in your life and point to some resources to help you.

In 1976, a couple of months before the United States celebrated its Bicentennial, Johnny Cash had his last chart-topping hit with a song about stealing parts from the GM plant where the song narrator worked to assemble himself a Cadillac for free. He was going to take them "one piece at a time." In the end, the assembled car was a mix of parts from about 25 different model years. It didn't look great. He and his buddies had to use an "A-daptor kit" to make it all fit together, but in the end, his wife liked it enough that she wanted him to take her for a spin.

We humans aren't that much different from Johnny's Cadillac. We are a mixture of our genetics, our early history, our current experiences, and environment. We are assembled, one piece at a time, over many years, and very often look like we were bolted together from mismatched parts. We may not look like much, but, if we're lucky, those we love want to take us for a spin.

Why is it that when we have some mismatched parts, we think it will be easy to make a change? We read a book we enjoy or see a compelling video; we get all hot and bothered about being motivated to change. We look in the mirror. We do some affirmations we learned from our 7th grade health teacher. We resolve to transform our lives . . . and not a damn thing ever changes. Then we feel even worse than when we started. How do we ever change?

An Over-Eager Student

I've been in the change-making business ever since I got my degree in 1991. I owe a tremendous debt of gratitude to all my teachers. Training to be a psychologist in graduate school is a mixture of types of learning. We had classroom lectures to learn things like neurobiology (one of my favorites), at least a year of statistics, tests and assessments, and research methods.

Those classes made us think like scientists. We also had a bunch of ex-periential classes—for example, ones where we became the clients in a therapy group. Those usually made me feel uncomfortable. The ones that helped me become good at the practice of psychotherapy, counseling, and coaching were called "practica." These classes were really apprenticeships. In these classes we practiced our skills on real people. In my first counsel-ing practicum, our team of teachers watched us like hawks. And well they should have. We had no idea what we were doing.

Each counseling room had a one-way mirror, a camera to record the in-teraction on VHS tape, with a teacher watching our session in real time. If things ever got squirrely, one of our teachers would be just down the hall ready to run in and rescue us from our mistakes. At the end of each session, we watched the tape of our counseling interaction and took notes. Then each week, we met with one or two teachers to go over the same hour of tape. (I've got to tell you, there isn't much more boring than watching yourself have the same hour-long conversation three times in a week. If you were a narcissist at the beginning, you eventually would get sick of watching yourself sit in an overstuffed chair between two ferns and listening to yourself talk.)

Each of us was assigned three clients to see during the 10-week academic quarter. We started with an intake interview, where we were to gather as much information as possible. Then, after consulting with one of the instructors, we began work the second week with our clients.

My professor for my first practicum was Rich Russell, a remarkably skilled therapist, wise and funny, and a genuinely decent man. My very first client was an 18-year-old woman in her first year of college. After having repeatedly watched myself on videotape talking to this young lady, I had my second session with her. Rich was poised down the hall to rescue her from my novice interventions if the need arose. At the end of the 50-minute hour, I had my first meeting with Rich.

His first question was, "So, Roger, what's your plan?"

Being good at school, I knew I had this answer locked up. I had a plan. What else was I going to do while watching myself on video for three hours? I had divided our next eight weeks up in line with my plan. I told Rich I'd work on one issue for two weeks, a second issue for three weeks, then her final issue for two weeks. Then we'd have our closing session and I'd launch her into a successful life. I was feeling pretty fat and sassy.

Rich paused for what seemed like a really long time (and here I'm going to give you the edited version of what Rich said, because this is a PG-rated book) and said, "Roger, it took her 18 years to get screwed up. Don't think you can fix her in eight weeks."

(But he didn't say "screwed" nor did he say "fudged." Rich didn't work " . . . in profanity the way other artists might work in oils or clay," but he could drop an occasional atomic bomb for effect. That day he did—and he made his point. I've remembered it for over 30 years.)

My problem, starting out, was that I believed people were almost as easy to fix as a broken lamp. Rich was right. Her mindset habits had taken 18 years to form. There was no way she would be able to change those four-lane neural superhighways of bad thought habits in eight weeks. We didn't know it at the time, but we were fighting against biology. It was going to take a lot longer than that.

People are not so easy to change, after all. Since you, dear reader, qualify as a person, your bad habits of thought and behavior are not easy to change either. Give yourself a little grace. Reading this book is the first step toward the lasting change you are looking for.

Remember that your changed thought patterns will change your brain's physiology and biochemistry.

It will take time and practice, practice, practice.

One Thing at a Time

Like Johnny Cash stealing car parts, you need to change only one thing at a time. In his book, *The Power of Habit*, Charles Duhigg introduced the concept of *keystone habits*. As humans, if we try to change too many things, we never change anything. We get distracted by the options for change and never get forward motion on any of them.

Duhigg's advice is to change one thing at a time. So how do you choose which thing to change? His advice is to pick a *small win*. Look for a *small win* and build on that. Don't swing for the fences—just get to first base.

Once you get some momentum going, and your *keystone habit* is well and truly engrained, *then and only then* do you add another.

I have a client who made a change in his organization's work habits. He said, "We have to make it like breathing." Once you have made the *keystone habit* as regular and mindless as breathing, then move onto the next habit you want to change.

"Education Without Execution Is Just Entertainment"

I start and end almost every one of my public presentations with this quote from Tim Sanders the author of *Love is the Killer App*: "Education without execution is just entertainment." With his alliteration, he has memorably encapsulated what makes people change.

Now that you're nearly done with this book, I hope you have enjoyed it. I hope you chuckled here and there while reading it. I hope that when you see an old Western or see a Volkswagen Beetle, or hear a song, or grab a Slurpee at 7-Eleven, it sparks a **novel reminder** to help you change your mindset and your life. The purpose was to plant enough of these story reminders in your head so you can't help but change. I hope to have made it *stupid easy* to change your thinking.

But if you want to supercharge your brain change, it's going to take work and practice. You've got to execute a decision and action.

Execution Step

Here's where you need to get active with this book. Grab a pen or highlighter and go through each chapter summary where you've written out what habit you want to change and what your **Mental Monkey** will be. Circle or highlight the few that are going to be *"small wins."* Review the ones you've circled. Then choose. I want you to write out which ONE of those habits you're going to change right now.

The **ONE** *keystone habit* I'm going to change first:

_____

_____

_____

_____

Which **Mental Monkey** am I going to set up to remind me of my new mental habit? (If you'd like, buy a Barrel of Monkeys, and slip one of the monkeys in your pocket as an **irritating reminder** for this step).

_____

_____

_____

_____

_____

Which musician and song will live rent-free in your head for this *keystone habit*?

_____

_____

_____

_____

_____

_____

Write out some additional songs for your *DIY Brain* Playlist to help with this change. Set them up on your computer, phone, or streaming service. Make it your drive-time playlist, your exercise jam, or your lunch hour Mindset Makeover Mixtape.

_____

_____

_____

_____

_____

You're on your way!

But wait, there's more . . .

References

Duhigg, C. (2012). *The Power of Habit: Why We Do What We Do and How to Change.* Random House.

Sanders, T. & Stone, G. (2003). *Love Is the Killer App: How to Win Business and Influence Friends.* Currency.

ADDITIONAL RESOURCES

Your **mindset makeover** is your responsibility, but every little bit helps. Here are some other resources I've created to help you.

First, go to DIYBrain.net. There you'll find links to all these resources.

Mindset Makeover Movies Bonus Chapter

At DIYBrain.net you can get access to the bonus chapter: *Mindset Makeover Movies*. You'll get access to a list of my favorite movies that can inspire, entertain, and change your brain forever. I'll tell you what to look for in each movie and why I recommend it.

Staying Happy Being Productive: The Big 10 Things Successful People Do— This is an airplane read or listen. If you start reading the book during the preflight instructions, you'll probably be done before you reach your destination. If you prefer to listen, download it before you head to the airport for your vacation and by the time you hit the beach, you'll have listened to it all. At the end, you'll have learned the 10 things successful people do.

Expedition – If you have the leadership bug and want to work through a leadership manual on your own or with a group of like-minded people, this guidebook will help you build the internal structures to become a strong leader. Available at CompassConsultation.com.

Daily Dose of Mental Marinade – Each day the Daily Dose helps you soak in something different from what you'll get from the news. The longer you soak in the marinade, the more you take on its flavor. Each day you'll get a quote designed to help you replace your head trash with better stuff. You also can sign up to get it via email on DrRogerHall.com or follow me at Twitter or Instagram @Rogers2Cents.

@Rogers2Cents – Each week, *Roger's 2 Cents* is a video, blog, or podcast that is designed to help you with your mindset makeover. If you want to receive it in your email, you can also sign up at DrRogerHall.com. Find *Roger's 2 Cents* on Twitter or Instagram by following @Rogers2Cents.

Subscribe to the *DrRogerHall* YouTube channel and get the weekly update. You can see the *DIY Brain* Mindset Makeover Music Playlist there to see what music changes my thinking and mood. You'll also see an extensive library of my training videos.

Follow *DIY Brain* on Facebook and post your DIY Playlists for others to see. You can help others by showing them what has worked for you. Tell your friends and share the stories in this book that are helping you change your life. It feels great to know you are helping someone else have a better life.

If you're prone to worry, learn more about your own levels of worry by taking the Worryometer Quiz at WorryOMeter.com.

Do you want to know how you react when you're afraid? Take the Freak Out! Quiz at FreakOutQuiz.com.

If it turns out that you've got a worry problem, check out the online course: Freak Out! Fear Less, Live More at FreakOutCourse.com.

The Freak Out! course is over 10 hours of training on:

- Why you never want to get rid of fear
- Why fear is good
- Why worry is bad

- What fear does to your body
- What kinds of things people fear
- How to get over your fears
- What you can do to replace those fears with productive action
- How to live a more fulfilled life

Musical Coda—A Couple More for the DIY Brain Playlist

I'll finish where I started. I listened to Johnny Cash while writing much of *DIY Brain* and the conclusion (One Piece at a Time) is named after one of his songs. So, it only makes sense that we finish our *DIY Brain* Mental Makeover Mixtape with two last songs:

One Piece at a Time – Johnny Cash

Johnny Cash – Lenny Kravitz; Lenny's love song which turns out to be an homage to Johnny Cash and June Carter.

Great Books to DIY Your Brain (Not Already Listed)!

Amen, D.G. (2012). *Use Your Brain to Change Your Age (Enhanced Edition): Secrets to Look, Feel, and Think Younger Every Day.* Potter/TenSpeed/Harmony.

Amen, D.G. (2013). *Unleash the Power of the Female Brain: Supercharging Yours for Better Health, Energy, Mood, Focus, and Sex.* Harmony.

Diamandis, P.H. & Kotler, S. (2012). *Abundance: The Future Is Better Than You Think.* Simon and Schuster.

Dweck, C.S. (2008). *Mindset: The New Psychology of Success.* Random House Digital, Inc.

Fredrickson, B. (2009). *Positivity.* Harmony.

Haidt, J. (2006). *The Happiness Hypothesis: Finding Modern Truth in Ancient Wisdom.* Basic Books.

Kotler, S. (2021). *The Art of Impossible: A Peak Performance Primer.* HarperCollins.

McKeown, G. (2020). *Essentialism: The Disciplined Pursuit of Less.* Currency.

Ridley, M. (2010). *The Rational Optimist: How Prosperity Evolves.* New York: HarperCollins.

Rubin, G. (2009). *The Happiness Project.* New York: HarperCollins.

Seligman, M.E. (2012). *Flourish: A Visionary New Understanding of Happiness and Well-Being.* Simon and Schuster.

Seligman, M.E. (2002). *Authentic Happiness: Using the New Positive Psychology to Realize Your Potential for Lasting Fulfillment.* Simon and Schuster.

Tierney, J. & Baumeister, R.F. (2021). *The Power of Bad: How the Negativity Effect Rules Us and How We Can Rule It.* Penguin.

ACKNOWLEDGMENTS

Kevin Harris and the Harris Harper Foundation for early support on this project. Thank you for taking a risk on an unknown author. Thank you also for your patience over these years and your editorial insight. I am glad to finally be able to place this book in your hands and share the message with the world.

Jamie Bryant and Joanne Grote on early edits. Jamie on advice and wisdom about the book business. You gave me a good start. Thank you.

Maryanna Young, Jennifer Regner, Beth Berger, and the rest of the team at Aloha whose constant encouragement restarted this project. The manuscript was fermenting in a file drawer for decades. Thank you for helping me dust it off to share it with the world.

Ted Knapke for initial cover design and interior concept. You'll probably never meet an easier person to work with than Ted.

Brad Gibson who initially encouraged me to write the book based on a series of talks I gave at Northwest Chapel Grace Brethren Church in Dublin, Ohio. Thank you to the staff and elders of Northwest Chapel for the job that allowed me to gather these stories together and then the chance to test them out on some of the church members.

Howard and Jean Schmitt and the leaders of Sharon Mennonite Church in Plain City, Ohio, who sponsored the second public presentation of these ideas.

Bev and L.H. Newcomb for letting me stay at their lake house to write the original manuscript ("Only at the lake!"). A special thank you, Bev, for your patient proofreading of this and hundreds of my other documents. I am grateful to have been able to work with you for over 25 years.

Johnny Cash, whose music was the soundtrack of the first draft of this book. In 2001 or 2002, Bev and L.H. left a Johnny Cash cassette at their lake house while I was there. I played Johnny's tape over and over for the three days I spent writing. Before then, I hadn't cared for his music, or any country music for that matter. Over the course of the next few years, I began to enjoy a whole genre of music I had never known. Johnny is in heavy rotation on my playlist.

To all the other musicians living rent-free in my head. Thank you for changing my brain.

To my professors who trained me to become a psychologist. Lyle Schmidt and Rich Russell, described in this book; Ted Kaul, who taught me more in the hallway (with whatever was on the top of his mind) than many professors ever taught their students in hours of classwork; to the other professors in my program: Sam Osipow, Nancy Betz, Bruce Walsh, Don Dell, Pamela Highlen, and Martin Heesacker, my sincere gratitude.

Two other professors deserve a special note. I took one undergraduate and two graduate neuropsychology courses from Gary Berntson. He was one of the more difficult and exceptional professors I had in my years at Ohio State. Along with John Cacioppo, Dr. Berntson pioneered the field of social neuroscience. He gave me the foundational understanding of the brain that has guided the rest of my career. One of my regrets is that I didn't take more courses from him. While in grad school, I was befriended by Michael Torello, a leading-edge neuroscience researcher in Ohio State's Department of Psychiatry. What I didn't learn from Dr. Berntson I learned over coffee with Mike. Both men are among the top five smartest people I know (I'm not even among the top 100 smartest people I know). Anything I get right in this book is because of these two men. Anything I get wrong in this book is my own fault. Drs. Berntson and Torello: thank you for opening up a world to me.

ACKNOWLEDGMENTS

To my friends who read early drafts and gave me constructive feedback. That was enough to believe there was a reason to keep working at this project.

To the hundreds of clients who opened their lives to me and gave me a chance to teach them how to change their mindsets and brains through stories.

To my wife, Patty, my sister, Laura, and my children Sam, Luke, and Grace—for patiently and supportively watching this project through its inception, hibernation, and reemergence. Thank you.

To my parents, George and Carol Hall, to whom I owe so much. I am glad you are now whole and happy in heaven.

ABOUT THE AUTHOR

Dr. Roger Hall is a business psychologist, author, consultant, and speaker. He has one trick: he trains leaders to monitor and manage their thinking. Roger received his doctorate in psychology from Ohio State University in 1991. He has owned Compass Consultation, Ltd., a peak performance business psychology company, since 1999.

His clients are entrepreneurs, professionals, and business owners. He is especially qualified to help entrepreneurs and business owners become better leaders and find meaning, purpose, and happiness in their lives. Roger has worked with leaders from little companies with only a few people all the way up to behemoths that dominate their industries. He helps leaders become better versions of themselves so they can lead their people better.

He and his wife, Patty, live outside Boise, Idaho. He is grateful to be the father of three: Sam, Luke, and Grace.

Soli Deo gloria.

Other books by Dr. Roger Hall:

Staying Happy, Being Productive: The Big 10 Things Successful People Do

Expedition

CONNECT

If something in this book gave you an ah-ha moment, I would love to hear about it. I would be very grateful if you would be willing to post a review on Amazon.

Connect with Roger Hall on LinkedIn

Like @Compass Consultation, Ltd. on Facebook

Follow @Rogers2Cents on Twitter and Instagram

To let me know about your successes, inquire about a speaking event for your organization, or learn about you or your company working with me, write me at support@DrRogerHall.com.

God bless!

DIYBrain.net
DrRogerHall.com
CompassConsultation.com

Made in the USA
Middletown, DE
03 June 2023

31979342R00149